Congress Declares War

Congress Declares War

RHETORIC, LEADERSHIP, AND PARTISANSHIP IN THE EARLY REPUBLIC

Ronald L. Hatzenbuehler

and

Robert L. Ivie

The Kent State University Press

Copyright © 1983 by The Kent State University Press, Kent, Ohio 44242
All rights reserved.
Library of Congress Catalog Card Number 83-8996
ISBN: 0-87338-292-7
Manufactured in the United States of America

Library of Congress Cataloging in Publication Data

Hatzenbuehler, Ronald L.
   Congress declares war.

   Bibliography: p.
   Includes index.
   1. United States—History—War of 1812—Causes. 2. United States. Congress—History—19th century. 3. War, Declaration of—Case studies. I. Ivie, Robert L. II. Title.
E357.H28 1983   973.5'21   83-8996
ISBN 0-87338-292-7

To
Linda and Nancy

Contents

Tables and Figures

Preface

This book has a strange history. The authors became acquainted socially at Idaho State University during the 1974–75 academic year through mutual friends. Seldom did we have substantive discussions about any academic subject, much less the War of 1812. Then, at a farewell party for the Ivies, we began to discuss the idea behind this book, i.e., that a historian and a rhetorician might together have something new to contribute to an understanding of the war crises of the early Republic.

The first step toward writing the book involved separate presentations on the same panel at the Western Speech Communication Convention in 1976. Ivie's paper focused on prowar rhetoric in 1812; Hatzenbuehler's provided a rationale for why historians and rhetoricians would want to collaborate in studying the origins of that war. The following year, for the Pacific Coast Branch of the American Historical Association, we collaborated on a joint paper focusing on the issue of war justification, subsequently published in *Social Science History*. Independently, audiences at the Organization of American Historians, Northern Great Plains History Conference, Pacific Coast Branch AHA (again), Eastern Communication Association, Pacific Northwest American Studies Association, and Western Speech Communication Association (again) have heard papers from the authors testing the methods and conclusions of the book. Finally, by mail, phone, and too infrequent visits to Pocatello or Pullman, we have put the final product together.

We pursue in this book a new avenue of research into the tangled question of why nations declare war, through the specific example of the War of 1812. Rather than approach this question by searching for still another uncharted cause of that war, we have determined to bridge a gap between present knowledge of causal agents and continuing uncertainties over how they were activated. To arrive at a better understanding of *why*, we have shifted attention from what caused the war to *how* it was declared. By examining the catalysts of war, we go beyond a static analysis of latent forces to explore the principal dynamics of the process of declaring war—a process whereby multiple possibilities and potentialities were eventually narrowed to a single choice. The final decision for war may seem in retrospect to have been the inevitable result of ideology, economics, or other underlying causes. In fact, it was the product of a group's search for a viable option among alternative courses of action. Our study investigates how congressmen in 1812 defined their options and agreed upon the particular solution of war.

To specify how Republicans reached their prowar decision, we develop a model comprised of the three main components of a congressman's behavior: voting, speaking and writing, and interacting with others. Voting behavior is addressed by charting how partisanship affected roll call votes. Language behavior is studied by attending to the topics and structure of rhetoric. Contacts among legislators are identified by considering leadership networks. Finally, interactions of these behavioral components are discovered by modeling the relationships among them.

It is important for readers to understand that we did not intend to create a model of congressmen's actions in the war session when we began to study how the Congress declared war in 1812. Only as we became convinced that we could define the process by which congressmen moved toward war did we think in terms of modeling the situation prowar congressmen faced. Based upon what we knew of what prowar congressmen *did*, we challenged ourselves to specify *how* they accomplished their task. Therefore, we view modeling as heuristic, serving as a preventative against over-simplification and hasty generalization and as a guide to further research. Throughout the book, we have tried to maintain this productive tension between the current status of knowledge and the continuing need for inquiry.

Beginning with an assessment of where historical literature on the War of 1812 stands, we introduce in chapter 1 our model of decision making. Chapters 2 through 4 explain how the three components of the model—leadership, partisanship, and rhetoric— combined to produce the nation's first war decision. Chapters 5 and

6 use the model as a perspective from which to view two additional early war crises during John Adams's and Thomas Jefferson's administrations, where the interaction of the same components that led to the war decision in 1812 failed to produce a similar result. Chapters 7 and 8 show how changes in policy, partisanship, and rhetoric between 1809 and 1811 set the stage for Madison's and the House leadership's more aggressive moves in the first session of the Twelfth Congress. Chapter 9 suggests how our study of the Congress in this period relates to other inquiries of the early Republic, especially regarding research on how republicanism informed people's behavior.

In composing the book, we have avoided jargon, but certain word choices that may be alien or awkward to readers are inevitable. Terms such as "model," "rhetor," or "behavioral component" are integral to the argument and endemic to interdisciplinary research. It may be that we have gained more from working together to produce this book than the readers will, but we hope not. We are convinced that there is a need for studies like this one. If scholars are to gain a fuller understanding of congressional behavior, they must begin with the realization that the Congress's actions are a function of legislators' speaking, voting, and interacting with one another. During the second session of the Tenth Congress, Massachusetts Representative Josiah Quincy put the matter this way:

> When we attempt to penetrate into the intentions of men, we are all sensible how thick and mysterious is that veil, which, by the law of our nature, is spread over them. At times it is scarcely permitted to an individual to be absolutely certain of his own motives. But when the question is concerning the purposes of others, experience daily tells how hard a task it is to descend into the hidden recesses of the mind, and pluck intentions from that granite cell, in which they delight to incrust themselves. The only mode of discovery is to consider language and conduct, in their relation to the real and avowed object, and thence to conclude, as fairly as we can, which is the one, and which the other. This course I shall adopt.[1]

Using different methods from those Quincy might have envisioned, we have tried to accomplish the same task.

1. [Annals of Congress.] *Debates and Proceedings in the Congress of the United States, 1789–1824* (Washington, D.C.: Gales and Seaton, 1853), 10th Cong., 2nd sess.: 1107–8. Henceforth referred to as *Annals of Congress.*

Many people have greatly assisted in the preparation of this book for publication. Lawrence S. Kaplan has had a hand in every phase of its development, and we are especially grateful for his valuable suggestions, criticisms, and undaunted advocacy. Robert P. Swierenga has afforded us advice and aid of the most helpful sort. Norman K. Risjord's review of the complete manuscript provided encouragement and ample opportunities for revision. J. C. A. Stagg's insights into Madison and the early national period have been especially stimulating. Special thanks are also extended to Jo Ann Ruckman, who read an early draft of the book, and Laura Nagy and Paul H. Rohmann, each of whom challenged us to write through jargon and greatly improved our word choices.

Throughout the several years it took us to put the book together, many helpful suggestions were also offered by commentators at professional meetings, most notably Roger H. Brown, Noble E. Cunningham, Walter R. Fisher, Harry W. Fritz, and Andrew A. King. Portions of chapters previously published in the *William and Mary Quarterly, Pacific Historical Review, Social Science History, Quarterly Journal of Speech*, and *Communication Monographs* are reworked herein with permission of the editors of these journals. The roll call data were supplied by the Inter-University Consortium for Political and Social Research, which bears no responsibility for our conclusions. Washington State University facilitated the project considerably with a grant of professional leave, and the Faculty Research Committee of Idaho State University supported our work with grant number 471.

Finally, we want to acknowledge the special contributions of our wives to this undertaking. Without their patience, love, and good will, the book would never have been completed. For all of these reasons, and more, we dedicate it to them.

CHAPTER ONE

Beyond the "Republican Synthesis"

The Need for a Dynamic Model of Decision Making in 1812

In the four decades since Warren H. Goodman summarized the major causes of the War of 1812, two major shifts in interpretive stance have moved research on the war question into areas Goodman could never have foreseen. First, economic and sectional interpretations popularized by George Rogers Taylor and Julius W. Pratt have given way in recent years to political interpretations of the war's declaration. Early in the war session, the Republicans molded a consensus favoring a declaration of war and, as the session wore on, successfully suppressed potentially disruptive pressures from within or outside their ranks to insure the passage of their war measures. By June of 1812, the war issue had become so thoroughly entangled with partisan political strategies that saving the Republican party was equated with the goal of saving the republican nation.[1]

Second, as a result of this shifting emphasis the period of time during which the primary causes for the war originated has been considerably expanded. No longer do scholars concentrate almost exclusively on the period after 1805 when the European wars became especially threatening to the United States. Refusing to label the War of 1812 as primarily an American response to European problems, historians since the 1960s have increasingly viewed the war as a defense of republicanism born in 1776 but tracing its origins to English politics of the 1640s, and beyond that period to the Renaissance. As John R. Howe has written, the War of 1812 completed the process of founding the republic and thereby closed "one of the major chapters in America's historical development."[2]

Both of these lines of thought have been united into one interpretation that Robert E. Shalhope has labeled "the republican synthesis."[3] This new historiography rests on the conviction that the

War of 1812 was fought to preserve the republic's existence, threatened internally by a faction bent on destroying virtue and externally by a country determined to destroy the young nation. The list of scholars who have contributed to the development of the republican synthesis is long and impressive: Cecilia M. Kenyon, Bernard Bailyn, Roger H. Brown, Gordon H. Wood, Richard Buel, J. G. A. Pocock, Drew R. McCoy, and Lance Banning. The work of this group has added much to our understanding of the political origins of the war, but this interpretation does not adequately resolve the puzzle of the war's causes any more than previous theories have.

Essentially, there are two problems with the republican synthesis position. First, books and articles treating themes of national honor, partisan politics, and the role of the president and congressional leaders in shaping the final war decision are too diverse to be lumped together. When Richard Hofstadter wrote a decade ago that historians were approaching consensus on the political origins of the War of 1812, he saw agreement where in fact there was—and still is—none.[4] Second, historians have never successfully addressed the problems of what the prowar legislators did in 1812 or how they did it. The speeches of congressmen have never been systematically studied, and such issues as leadership and the interactions between the executive and legislative branches have been over-simplified. In short, even when the republican synthesis is added to the usual list of the war's causes, one still has "the feeling that a truly satisfactory explanation for the outbreak of the war has eluded its students."[5]

In the early 1960s Norman K. Risjord first focused attention on the politics of prowar voting in the war Congress. Attacking Margaret K. Latimer's contention that the congressional elections of 1810 had brought into the Congress a clique of South Carolinians—John C. Calhoun, William Lowndes, and Langdon Cheves—who were primarily successful in reversing Jeffersonian pacifism, Risjord contended that the addition of a "war hawk" element to the Twelfth Congress was not so important as a gradual shift of seasoned Republican congressmen "to a vigorous defense of American neutral rights." The majority of the Republicans who voted for war, Risjord argued, were men who had been in the Congress for many years, and their prowar stance was determined not by the younger war enthusiasts but rather by "the realization that something [had to] be done to vindicate national honor."[6]

Bradford Perkins's detailed account of Anglo-American relations from 1805 to 1812 approached the issue of national honor from a different perspective than Risjord's, but Perkins arrived at a similar conclusion. Perkins wrote his book, he said, to emphasize what many historians had ignored: "such things as national pride, sensitivity, and frustration." In agreement with Risjord on the War Hawk question, Perkins stated that prowar zealots were a persistent but largely ineffective force in breaking the deadlock in Congress between Federalist opposition to restrictions against the British and Republican determination to continue peaceful coercion. He emphasized that a majority of Republicans moved toward the war decision slowly and harbored great misgivings about the prudence of their course, but were finally trapped by indecision, miscalculations, and lack of leadership. Once committed, Republicans found in the theme of "national honor" a means of rationalizing their prowar stance and of making their conduct appear consistent in the eyes of their constituents.[7]

For both Risjord and Perkins, therefore, Republicans in the end were motivated to declare war by causes other than those isolated by Goodman and previous scholars. The belief that the nation's honor was at stake in the conflict with Great Britain provided majority party Republicans with the issue that could break the deadlock in Congress and move the nation toward war. This theme of national honor, which subsumed all the other causes of the war that historians had previously isolated, was especially prevalent in the speeches of prowar congressmen, and Risjord and Perkins in their studies focused primarily on the debates of the war session and the private letters of congressmen. Such phrases in these sources as "national humiliation," "shame and indelible disgrace," and "a reproach to all nations" validated the accuracy of their interpretations.

Contemporaneously with Risjord's and Perkins's research, Roger H. Brown pursued the war's origins from a slightly different tack. Brown shared the belief that a majority of Republicans moved hesitatingly toward war but felt that something more than national honor was at stake for those who supported war. For Brown, the cause of the war did not reside in British provocations against the nation caused by the British Orders in Council. Rather, Republicans viewed their actions in 1812 in the same light as the defense of republicanism that had brought the party to power in 1800, and they saw the principle extending through the Constitution and the American Revolution, all the way back to John Winthrop's dream of building a "Citty upon a Hill." Republicans pursued war, Brown argued, as the only way to save their imperiled nation and to insure the success of the republican form of government.[8]

Brown also relied heavily on the private letters of congressmen, in many cases utilizing manuscript resources unconsulted by prior historians, to document his belief that shared fears concerning the permanence of the republican experiment in America motivated Republicans to declare war. In contrast to Risjord and Perkins, however, Brown was able to break away from views of the war that labeled it as an American response to foreign policy problems encountered since 1805. Brown contended that concerns for the viability of the republic that had motivated the leaders of the American Revolution were also central to those who favored war in 1812. Building upon the scholarship of Cecilia M. Kenyon and Bernard Bailyn for the Revolutionary period, Brown said that he hoped "these studies [would] reinforce each other and cumulatively form a coherent pattern of new interpretation in the history of the Revolutionary and early national periods."[9]

Brown's hopes have been realized through the work of half a dozen scholars who have filled the chronological gap that existed between Bailyn's and Brown's work. Gordon H. Wood extended the research of Kenyon and Bailyn into the 1780s with his study of the formation of the Constitution, *The Creation of the American Republic, 1776–1787*. According to Wood, those men who wrote the Constitution viewed republicanism as more than an abstraction. What made republics great and, at the same time, provided the key element in their downfall throughout history was the character and spirit of the people, expressed in terms of "public virtue." This virtue, manifested in frugality, temperance, industry, and simplicity, easily degenerated into chaos when people selfishly pursued their own ends rather than those that promoted the general welfare. In affirming the "sovereignty of the people," the founding fathers were, in Wood's view, locating both their hopes and fears for the future of the republic in the same place.[10]

John R. Howe's important article, "Republican Thought and the Political Violence of the 1790s" and Richard Buel, Jr.'s book, *Securing the Revolution: Ideology in American Politics, 1789–1815*, accomplished the same task as Wood for the 1790s and showed how safeguarding public virtue became a highly contentious undertaking. Both authors show how the "pervasive ideological attachment to the concept of republicanism" that formed the basis of the consensus motivating the founding fathers "promoted discord rather than harmony" among the leaders of the early Republic. Shared assumptions of the members of the Revolutionary generation concerning the establishment and maintenance of republicanism—chief of which was the "widespread belief in the essential frailty and impermanence of republican government"—were greatly intensified by fears of disruptive factions in the new nation. "Every decision they made," Howe concluded, "loomed as fundamentally important. Their opportunity, they firmly believed, could not be recovered." Concentrating specifically on the Republicans as they formed in opposition to Federalist policies in the 1790s, Buel showed how Republicans convinced themselves that government by their party provided "the only way to ensure that the nation would remain independent and the promise of the Revolution would be fulfilled."[11]

Most recently, J. G. A. Pocock, Drew R. McCoy, and Lance G. Banning have brought "the republican synthesis" into the early 1800s. The Renaissance notion that republics are temporary because the passage of time corrupts virtue had been largely discredited by the early Federalists' argument that the nation could be both large and republican. But during the 1790s, Alexander Hamilton and others in power succeeded in reviving old fears regarding the impermanence of a republican form of government. As Jefferson and Madison came to oppose Hamilton's manufacturing and mercantile economy with its attendant strong central government, "the Federalist-Republican controversy . . . [became] to a quite startling extent a replay of the debates of Court and Country as much as a hundred years before." Banning especially has shown convincingly how Jefferson helped "to create a party that would call itself Republican and rest to a remarkable degree on a revival and Americanization of British opposition thought [of the 1640s]." And McCoy, in *The Elusive Republic*, shows how old world debates that commerce destroys virtue were reborn in America during the early national period. "Above all," McCoy cautions, "American republicanism must be understood as an ideology in transition, for it reflected an attempt to cling to the traditional republican spirit of classical antiquity without disregarding the new imperatives of a more modern commercial society." Presumably, Banning's biography of Madison will chart the "Country party's" path to war in 1812—the final chapter in the republican synthesis position.[12]

So long as one traces the evolution of the idea of republican government through the various authors, few problems arise in accepting the legitimacy of the republican synthesis position. The validity of the argument breaks down, however, when one questions the extent to which republican ideology, so admittedly amorphous and constantly changing, *motivated* legislators to declare war in 1812. When one retraces the same argument already outlined but focuses instead on the problem of how Republicans used a defense of republicanism to guide their actions, the synthesis dissolves. Consider, in the first instance, Risjord's "national honor" and Brown's "imperiled nation" thesis. Ideologically speaking, one would be hard-pressed to distinguish between the two terms, but behaviorally they meant different things to the actors if one follows Risjord's and Brown's arguments carefully.

According to Risjord, it was a patriotic desire to vindicate the honor of the nation that eventually overcame the "Jeffersonian pacifism" long held by a majority of Republicans. Submission to Great Britain would mean, in Risjord's terms, "national disgrace," and those men who voted for war did so "primarily to defend their rights, not their purses." In Brown's analysis, however, power considerations play a much more prominent role. Great Britain from the outside and Federalists from within were subverting republicanism, and only a declaration of war would save the republic. Indeed, it was questionable in the minds of many Federalists and Englishmen whether a republican form of government could declare and successfully wage a war. Thus, however reluctantly the majority of Republicans moved toward war, in accomplishing their goal they hoped to ensure the continuation of the republican form of government. In short, Risjord and Brown stressed different motivational factors in explaining why Republicans declared war.[13]

Similarly, although there are many points in common between Risjord's and Perkins's views, essential differences regarding the use of a national honor rationale for war have never been satisfactorily resolved. Whereas Risjord argued that defending the nation's honor was a sincerely held belief of most Republicans, Perkins labeled the national honor argument as a "rationalization" for essentially irrational behavior. Neither moderates in the Congress nor the president nor his advisors could control the situation, and only after the War Hawks seized the day and successfully moved the nation toward war did the national honor thesis surface. And even then, Republicans invented the argument in order to make their actions appear to be consistent when in fact they were not. In rhetorical terms, Risjord viewed the national honor theme as a persuasive technique used to win supporters for the war. Perkins saw it as *ex post facto* camouflage for specious reasoning. Therefore, Gordon Wood may be right, in part, when he says that by reading Risjord and Brown (and Perkins) one will receive "the best perspective on the logic of the Republicans' foreign policy that led to war," but it is also true that substantive differences in the positions still require attention.[14]

Not only have historians glossed over these differences, but republican synthesists have also given disproportionate weight to Republican theorists. As Shalhope has pointed out, "It is a mistake to interpret Thomas Jefferson as the champion of republicanism and his Federalist opponents as its great foes. To do so is to accept only Jefferson's version of the argument."[15] The work of David H. Fischer, Linda K. Kerber, Gerald Stourzh, and James H. Banner, Jr., establish the fact that safeguarding the republican experiment was also central to the ideology of the Federalists from the 1790s until 1812.[16] Especially revealing in this regard is Banner's book, *To the Hartford Convention*. Banner shows how both Republicans and Federalists believed in the 1780s and 1790s that they were saving the republic. They simply disagreed on how to do it. To Federalists, "the question of an American despotism seemed no less relevant . . . [after 1800] than the issue of monarchy had seemed thirty years before. . . . Where for the most ardent Republicans the growth of social and political democracy had become the symbol of a revolution achieved, for the Federalists of Massachusetts it stood as the hallmark of a revolution corrupted—and, for some of them, an encouragement to a new revolution." By 1814, Federalists viewed the Republican-dominated national government as equal to the ministry at Whitehall at the time of the American Revolution: "distant, alien, determined upon obedience, and heedless of the public will."[17]

Similarly, those men who called themselves Republicans but refused increasingly after 1805 to follow the lead of the administration in domestic and foreign policy matters also based their actions on a defense of republicanism. James M. Garnett, Richard Stanford, John Taylor of Caroline, and especially John Randolph viewed the actions of Jefferson, Madison and Albert Gallatin as a declension from the ideals of the American Revolution and the "Revolution of 1800." These "Old Republicans," or Quids, saw the world of the early Republic in clear and simple terms: "Love of peace, hatred of offensive war, jealousy of the State Governments toward the General Government; a dread of standing armies; a loathing of public debt, taxes, and excise; tenderness for the liberty of the citizen; jealousy, Argus-eyed jealousy, of the patronage of the President." Randolph and the others did not form a new political party but rather reveled in their extreme isolation from the disastrous policies—in their eyes—of the nation's leaders. They enjoyed their position because it confirmed their conviction that the Anglo-American legacy of republican government was being destroyed by both the Federalists and the Republicans. As Randolph put it in 1805, "I practise the doctrines now that I practised in 1798. Gentlemen may hunt up the journals if they please; I voted against all such projects under the Administration of John Adams, and I will continue to do so under that of Thomas Jefferson."[18]

If all the political leaders of early America were motivated by the same ideological concerns, an exclusive emphasis on the preservation of republicanism as encompassing the political origins of the War of 1812 is misguided. As Shalhope has stated, republicanism remained a vague and supple concept which represented only a general consensus against aristocracy and monarchy, and "beyond this, agreement vanished." Instead of making the republican synthesis "a drug on the historical market," we need to know how each group translated the abstract notion of republicanism into concrete behaviors. Even if Republicans, Quids, and Federalists shared a consensus about the need to preserve the republican form of government, they acted differently in defending it.[19]

The second problem with the "republican synthesis," as with all the standard justifications for the war, is that it cannot meaningfully address one of the most perplexing issues relating to the War of 1812—its timing. Even if one could devise the perfect weighting of factors leading to war, why it occurred in 1812 would still remain obscure. Each of the major factors historians have identified as being most important in leading to war—Indian attacks on the frontier, economic dislocation resulting from the Napoleonic wars, violation of the rights of neutral nations in time of war, insults to national pride and honor, and domestic political feuding between Republicans and Federalists—were present in varying degrees since the 1790s and cannot, therefore, be said to have determined war in 1812. Indeed, very strong cases can be made that war should have come at many points during the Adams or Jefferson presidencies when depredations on commerce and wounded national pride were more directly encountered—in 1798 or 1807, for example—and should not have come in 1812 when the press of events was not nearly so intense. What is needed is an explanation of why the factors that best explain the war's outbreak—factors occurring over various periods of time—all came together when they did. Therefore, instead of a static analysis that sifts out the component parts of the decision for war by isolating the war's causes, in this study we have constructed a model of the dynamics behind the movement to war.

In building our model of decision making in 1812, we have concentrated on the behavior of the Congress not only because of the constitutional requirement that Congress declare war but also because it was in this arena that the nation worked out the justification for a declaration of war. We have focused attention on the House of Representatives because that is where most of the war legislation originated in 1811–12 and because it was on the floor of the House that the rationale for war developed. For some of the nation's leaders in 1812, the suspense probably was "hell" (as Leland R. Johnson has portrayed the Senate's consideration of the war declaration), but the conviction remains after studying both groups that the Senate probably would have gone along with whatever the House had decided.[20]

Behaviorally speaking, the actions of congressmen in 1812 may be organized into three functions: they voted, they spoke and wrote, and they interacted with one another. The votes of congressmen are important because they are the official record of the legislators' choices among concrete issues. Because the votes are available in machine-readable format, computer-detected trends in voting help the researcher to reconstruct the alternatives congressmen faced when they cast their votes. Likewise, debates and circular letters to constituents constitute a significant part of a legislator's public record where important clues to the speaker's motives may be found. Unfortunately, contemporary public address has jaded many researchers to the importance of the spoken word for earlier political leaders who felt the necessity of justifying their actions to their constituents. In early America, speechmaking and letter writing were important functions of a congressman during his tenure in the nation's capital.

Many of a legislator's actions, however, occurred in private settings. Committee meetings in the early Congress were very informal affairs conducted in private offices or at a congressman's living quarters. Similarly, not all the letters that a representative wrote were meant for public print or hearing, and the researcher must take care to check the private against the public utterances. Also, where a person lived; with whom he ate, drank, or attended social gatherings; who his (or his wife's) relations were; how close he stood to the administration or party leaders in the states; or simply with whom he happened to sit on the floor of the House often exercised a profound influence on his actions.

A dynamic model of congressional behavior, therefore, must not only consider what the legislators did (vote, speak, and interact with one another), but also attend to both the public and private settings within which the representatives operated. In other words, the situation in which the behaviors occurred was as important as the components of the legislator's actions, and out of the interaction between the situation and the concrete behaviors comes an understanding of the process of decision making that produced the War of 1812. Specifically, voting in the public forum produced a partisan record of behavior; speaking and writing, publicly and in private, developed a rhetorical justification for war; and informal relationships constructed the network of leadership through which decision making progressed.

With regard to voting, one must begin with the fact that party affiliation was the best predictor of the behavior of congressmen from John Adams's administration through the war session. Occasionally sectional, ideological, or other considerations may have influenced voting, but it was within a partisan context that the war crises of early America were resolved. But there are two problems with prior analyses of party voting during this period. First, the techniques of roll-call analysis give the researcher few clues for explaining why partisan affiliation is the best interpretation of congressional behavior. Party labels have always been the single best clue to why congressmen vote the way they do, but whether party affiliation should be viewed as a link with other, perhaps more important determinants of behavior or as an end in itself is not yet clear.[21] Second, Rudolph M. Bell has shown that those congressional districts that supported the war in 1812 had been used to "winning" long before the final war votes.[22] Similarly, a study of congressional voting on foreign policy issues from 1796 through 1812 reveals that party pressures on congressmen were most intense during John Adams's administration when levels of partisanship far surpassed those attained during the war session. If partisanship did not lead to war when it was the strongest, it does not make much sense to spotlight it during the period leading to war.[23]

It is also interesting to note, with respect to the studies dealing with congressional voting in the period, that they have failed to analyze speaking as an equally important component of congressional behavior. Bell did not address the speeches of congressmen at all, and others have viewed speechmaking primarily from the perspective of whether the verbal record mirrored or masked the voting record.[24] Studies based almost solely on the written record, however, have fallen into a similar trap by concentrating far too heavily on the ideology of party positions. Words are important not only for the ideology they express but also for how they apply it to particular circumstances. The verbal behavior of congressmen, both spoken and written, provides the most direct and detailed indication of how the legislators conceptualized the situation which the nation faced. The themes, arguments, and symbols congressmen used to construct and justify the war measures reveal a great deal about the hierarchies of beliefs and attitudes that they brought to bear on the decision-making process. And a close attention to the rhetoric through which these hierarchies were articulated and applied to the events of the day helps us to understand better the key steps through which a logic of war was formed.

But the main failing of previous studies, both of voting and of speaking, is that the way language and actions reinforced one another in the war session has been ignored. One must look at the relationships between voting and speaking in order to get a fuller view of congressional behavior. What distinguishes the 1811–12 period from earlier war crises is the way members of the majority party effectively coordinated words and actions. And out of this process of justifying their actions (voting and speaking) to themselves and to others, Republicans produced a declaration of war.

Finally, the leadership component of congressional behavior established the major behavioral link between executive and legislative branches of the government. Madison's personal and political problems came to a head in 1811–12 and inclined him toward an active role in the Twelfth Congress. During the war session, the president, Secretary of State James Monroe, Speaker of the House Henry Clay, and the House Foreign Relations Committee shared the leadership role, gave direction to the war movement, and shaped its content and timing. Meanwhile, behind the scenes influential congressmen lobbied effectively for the majority party's program.[25] Leaders in the House and the Executive branch, in other words, used partisan voting and a rhetorical justification as vehicles for moving the nation toward war.

In summary, partisanship, rhetoric, and leadership constitute the behavioral components of our model of decision making in the House in 1812. By focusing on these three aspects of what congressmen did and by probing how they did it, we believe it is possible to go beyond the republican synthesis and to understand the dynamics of the movement to war.

CHAPTER TWO

Model Building

The Leadership Component

In emphasizing the essential continuity of the period from the American Revolution through the War of 1812, republican synthesists have imposed a false unity on the events of the early national period. In order to construct a model of decision making that addresses systematically the movement toward war, it is first necessary to view the administrations of John Adams, Thomas Jefferson, and James Madison in some other way than simply as legacies of the American Revolution.

At the same time the leaders of the early republic were trying to continue the republican experiment and set precedents for public conduct in later periods, they were also forced to react to circumstances in order to understand the events of their time. Richard H. Kohn shows how the founding fathers attended mainly to the situations of the moment in creating the military establishment. Kohn's thesis, that the Federalists created the military establishment in order to save the republic from Republican antifederalism, reflects the strong influence of the republican synthesists on his thinking. What makes Kohn's study unique, however, is the emphasis he places on reconstructing the specific sequence of events leading to the creation of the standing army and navy. Such British opposition writers as John Trenchard viewed standing armies with horror, and these ideas informed the military philosophy of the Revolutionary generation. Bernard Bailyn, Gordon Wood, and Lance Banning make the same point. However, the experiences of the American Revolution, Kohn argues, reinforced later Federalists' dispositions toward "order, tradition, the natural distinctions among men, and social harmony" and by 1783 created a strong desire for a standing army. It was only in the late 1790s that Indian wars, the Whiskey

Rebellion, and Republican opposition caused Federalists to develop the beginnings of the modern system. Similarly, although he had opposed a *Federalist* army in the 1790s, Jefferson as president saw the need for at least some regular army personnel and in his first administration continued Federalist policies.[1]

Kohn, therefore, concerns himself less with tracing the development of the idea of a standing army than with interrelating the events that gave it life. J. C. A. Stagg pursues a method similar to Kohn's in studying Madison's economic coercion of Great Britain. Stagg argues that Madison as congressman, secretary of state, and president thought a great deal about the possibilities of coercing England to protect American mercantile interests. These thoughts did not revolve around the ideology of mercantilism or expansionism but rather were sharply focused on the British need to supply her colonies in the West Indies with staples. So long as the United States was the principal supplier of Great Britain, Madison felt economic coercion would force the English, however grudgingly, to respect American rights. But when he saw during his presidency that Canada had begun to replace the United States in the minds of policy makers in England, the future of economic coercion was thrown into jeopardy. Hence, the practical necessity of coping with the very threatening set of circumstances with regard to Canada should be weighted more heavily than his economic theories in explaining Madison's war decision.[2]

In both Kohn's and Stagg's studies, decision makers reacted more to the situation of the moment than from preconceived notions. This is not to say that ideas such as republicanism were not an important part of their thinking, only that ideology cannot be said to have caused specific actions. The situation determined the particular character of their actions far more than did considerations of ideological consistency. When applied directly to the issue of the timing of the declaration of war in 1812, this insight into understanding the situational components of decision making is instructive. Republicans in both the Congress and the executive branch were reacting in 1812 to what they perceived to be new sets of circumstances, not long-standing problems. This situational response becomes most apparent when one considers the situational components of leadership (this chapter), partisanship (chapter 3), and rhetoric (chapter 4).

Most historical studies of leadership are based on the premise that successful leaders possess certain personality traits that make them great. When sufficient admirable qualities are tallied, a man achieves greatness. But as black marks increase, leaders fall somewhere between "near great" and "failure." Additional subjective factors also color most "polls" concerning presidential greatness or assessments of leadership effectiveness. As Thomas A. Bailey has noted concerning A. M. Schlesinger's 1948 and 1962 polls of prominent students of the presidency, failure to control for "party biases, personal experiences, sectional prejudices, one's information or lack of it, one's philosophy of government, the findings of recent scholarship, new fashions in interpretation, and the current atmosphere" transforms the polling technique into "something of a parlor game" analogous to "pinning the tail on the donkey."[3]

Behavioral studies of leadership, conversely, suggest that a person's actions are determined more by the factors of the moment than by personality traits. By operationally defining behavior as a function of personality and environment, social psychologists place more emphasis on understanding the environment within which the action occurs than the personality of the actor. Of the environmental components influencing an action, the most important appears to be the "interpersonal relationship between the leader and his group members." Leaders are inseparable from the groups that they lead, and the group's desires and goals usually are more determinative of a leader's actions than his personality.[4]

There is one area of these leadership studies that seems most applicable to the problem of isolating those people in the Congress and the executive branch who were the leaders of the war movement in 1812. According to Paul F. Secord and Carl W. Backman, "There is growing empirical . . . and theoretical convergence . . . on considering as leadership behavior those acts that are functionally related either to goal achievement or to the maintenance and strengthening of the group."[5] Leaders, therefore, enable groups to attain a specific goal or perpetuation and cohesion. Concerning the war Congress, this view of leadership offers a new perspective from which to view the War Hawk question and to consider whether Madison was pressured into declaring war.

Few groups in early American history have captured the fancy of historians as have the War Hawks of 1812. They are mentioned in most textbooks, and each scholar writing about the origins of the War of 1812 has taken his turn at assessing their significance. In recent years, the vast majority of historians have portrayed them as the main war agents: a young, vociferous, aggressive, anti-British, optimistic, nationalistic, frontier-oriented, and small Republican faction that seized control of the House and Senate in late 1811; elected Henry Clay Speaker of the House; hammered out the major war legislation; and badgered President James Madison and harangued pacifist colleagues until Congress declared war. As Reginald Horsman concludes, "The true enthusiasts [for war] were remarkably few, but they were able to enlist a solid group of Republicans to vote with them on most of their measures and eventually obtained enough beyond this solid core to pass a declaration of war."[6]

While historians are in general agreement about the importance of the War Hawks as agents for war, there has been substantial disagreement on the role the group played in the Twelfth Congress. Characterizing the War Hawks as the best organized and most persistent of the many factions in the war session, Bradford Perkins stresses that their victory in June of 1812 was possible only because of the absence of alternative legislative or executive leaders. The War Hawks, in other words, won as much by default as by design. Similarly, Norman K. Risjord emphasizes that a desire to vindicate the nation's honor motivated a majority of the congressional Republicans to vote for war and that the War Hawks were chiefly catalysts rather than determining agents. There is even one student of the war's origins who denies the band any role in directing congressional deliberations. Characterizing the War Hawks as a "historical myth," Roger H. Brown argues that the private letters of the Republicans reveal no enthusiasm for war and that the majority of the party members viewed war as the only alternative to the destruction of the party and the republican experiment in America.[7]

In short, most scholars agree that there were War Hawks, but disagreement still exists concerning whether they led the Congress toward the war decision. Harry W. Fritz uses a model of influence based on political science theories to argue that a War Hawk faction worked actively behind the scenes to direct the House's deliberations in the war session.[8] There are two problems with such an analysis, however, in addressing whether the War Hawks were leaders in the movement toward war. First, Fritz's analysis of the War Hawks' activities is based on theories of how activists operate. These theories bear little relation to the voting behavior of the legislators. The single best criterion for isolating the War Hawks would seem to be a consistent voting pattern in support of war legislation. Regardless of the vitriolic speeches a congressman may give or letters he may write to constituents or hometown newspapers, he must follow through with his determination when the roll is called. Both Horsman's identification of War Hawks based upon "key" votes or Hatzenbuehler's analysis of the scalable war measures isolate southeastern, seaboard Republicans as forming the core of the War Hawk faction.[9] Fritz gives little attention to this or any other specific group of legislators. Second, Fritz views leadership from an *ad hoc* perspective and does not consider how the war legislation originated. When the question of War Hawk leadership is approached from the perspective of decision making in the Congress and the group orientation suggested above, an alternative conclusion is necessary. There were War Hawks, but Speaker of the House Henry Clay, the House Foreign Relations Committee, Secretary of State James Monroe, and President James Madison were primarily responsible for directing the war measures.

The best way to attack the leadership question is to determine which members dominated the legislation of the session.[10] Two representatives, Ezekiel Bacon of Massachusetts and Peter B. Porter of New York, introduced one-third of the Republican-sponsored legislation and the majority of the bills which carried the House (Table 2.1).[11] One might infer from this table that Bacon and Porter were extremely influential congressmen, but much of their power stemmed from the fact that they were chairmen of the important Ways and Means and Foreign Relations committees. Of these, the Foreign Relations Committee reported all of the legislation, except for the tax bills, on which a majority of Republicans agreed and was the most active committee of the House.[12]

With New Yorker Peter B. Porter as chairman, the Foreign Relations Committee included South Carolinian John C. Calhoun, Tennessean Felix Grundy, Virginian John Randolph, Kentuckian Joseph Desha, Pennsylvanian John Smilie, Ebenezer Seaver of Massachusetts, John A. Harper of New Hampshire, and Federalist Philip B. Key of Maryland.[13] Three of the members (Calhoun,

Table 2.1
Republicans Introducing Two or More Foreign Policy Bills:
Twelfth House, First Session

Representative	State	Number Introduced	Number Carried	Percent Success
Bacon, Ezekiel	Ma	22	20	90.9
Porter, Peter B.	NY	18	15	83.3
Randolph, John	Va	16	2	12.5
Williams, D. R.	SC	10	4	40.0
Cheves, Langdon	SC	5	5	100.0
Lacock, Abner	Pa	5	2	40.0
Grundy, Felix	Te	4	4	100.0
Rhea, John	Te	4	3	75.0
Roberts, Jonathan	Pa	4	3	75.0
Calhoun, John C.	SC	3	2	66.7
Wright, Richard	Md	3	1	33.3
Macon, Nathaniel	NC	2	0	0.0
Stanford, Richard	NC	2	1	50.0

Grundy, and Harper) were new to the Congress—a striking fact since only twenty-five of the freshman legislators (40 percent) received seats on committees, and half of that number were placed on the lowly Post Office and Postal Roads and Apportionment of Representatives committees.[14] Traditionally, historians have explained the committee assignments of Calhoun, Grundy, and Harper in terms of their youth and War Hawk vigor.[15] Admittedly, the three were active in floor debates, but other, more practical reasons may have been behind two of the appointments. In the Twelfth Congress, Speaker of the House Henry Clay determined the placement of majority party congressmen. Calhoun was a member of Clay's mess. If the Speaker wanted to influence the committee's deliberations, he would have as his spokesman someone whom he saw every day. As for Harper, the New Hampshire representative was well regarded by Governor William Plumer (who, while in the Senate, was at least an acquaintance of Clay) and the state's party leaders. Only Isaiah Green and another freshman representative (also from New Hampshire), Obed Hall, could match Harper's partisan voting record. Clay's choice was thus a wise one.[16]

Clay's influence in the selection process is also seen in the remaining membership of the committee. Each of the experienced Republicans, with the exception of Randolph, whose seniority probably entitled him to a prestigious committee, had a record of unswerving loyalty to the Republican party in previous Congresses. Joseph Desha and John Smilie, each of whom served on two committees, had been particularly active during the debates of the Eleventh Congress, although they had often disagreed with one another over policy decisions.[17] There is no record of a speech by Ebenezer Seaver during either the Eleventh or Twelfth congresses, but his support of the party position never wavered. The most enigmatic Republican on the committee was its chairman, Peter B. Porter. Based upon his voting record in past sessions (Table 2.2) Porter was a good risk. He was also an aggressive spokesman for the early war measures. However, he split with his colleagues over the timing of the war taxes, believing that money questions were premature. During the debates on the sixty-day embargo, Porter again dissented from the majority because he felt the war could not be fought with effect and because it would be "of immense injury to the State of New York, on account of their flour which has gone to market." Shortly after the embargo bill passed (the chairman voted against reading the bill a second time but for the final bill), Porter returned to his native state to organize the militia. In two soul-searching letters to Secretary of War William Eustis, Porter pleaded that the war be postponed until his part of the nation had prepared itself for the conflict. On June 4 he voted to delay the decision for war until the first Monday in October, but he either abstained or absented himself from the final war vote on that same day.[18]

Unfortunately, it is impossible on the basis of the few Foreign Relations Committee minutes which survive to determine conclusively who led the committee deliberations. Based upon their

Table 2.2
Republican Partisanship: Foreign Relations Committee, Twelfth House, First Session

	Percentage of Votes Against Party Majority on Foreign Policy Roll Calls			
Representative	*11 Cong., 1 sess.*	*11 Cong., 2 sess.*	*11 Cong., 3 sess.*	*12 Cong., 1 sess.*
Desha	14.3	17.5	6.9	11.3
Seaver	0.0	15.0	6.6	12.0
Smilie	0.0	18.4	9.1	17.3
Porter	28.6	12.3	6.8	32.2
Randolph	46.2	63.0	82.4	86.9

speeches and proposals, Grundy, Calhoun, Smilie, and (to a lesser extent) Harper stand out as the activists of the committee meetings. Desha and Seaver voted with the majority, but their levels of activity cannot be ascertained. Porter was a strong chairman and committee spokesman early in the session, and he faithfully carried out the committee's decisions even when he could no longer in good conscience follow the route he had helped to chart. Questioning mainly the timing of the war, he refused to join Key, a Federalist, or Randolph and other antiwar Republicans in direct opposition to the final war votes. Although the committee minutes leave in doubt the question of which member or members were most influential with their colleagues, it is clear that in framing the major war legislation of the session the committee did not work alone. Often the committee met in joint session with its Senate counterpart, and Speaker Clay was present at these joint meetings at least in the early part of the session.[19] But the person who worked most closely with the group was Secretary of State James Monroe.

At one of the first committee meetings in November 1811, Monroe pledged the administration's support for war in the spring of 1812 unless an "honorable peace" had by that time been worked out with the British. Writing to Andrew Jackson, Felix Grundy said the administration (through Monroe) had committed itself to a program which, if reversed, "will bring them down from their high places, If there be honest men enough to tell the truth loudly." At a February 6 meeting, Grundy moved that the committee direct the chairman to "address a letter to the Secretary of State requesting information in writing, whether the military force already provided by law is in the opinion of the Executive, competent to the purposes of national defence, & to the other objects contemplated by [the] Executive."[20] On February 11, Porter informed the committee that he had interviewed Monroe and that the Secretary had given the committee's letter to Madison. The president, however, had declined to give a written answer since he "deemed it a departure from the correct course of his official duties to hold formal & written communications with a committee of the house on the subject of the resolution." But the president did send a message through Monroe "that the Committee were already in possession of opinions of the Executive in respect to the number & species of troops proper to be provided, through the channel of informal communication hitherto pursued by the committee & the Executive."[21] The committee voted that no change was necessary.

The most important committee meetings of the session occurred in late March 1812. On March 24 and 30, Porter asked Monroe for the executive branch's feelings about an embargo (clearing the seas of American ships) as the first step toward war.[22] On March 31 Monroe met with the committee and said "the Executive was of the Same Opinion that it entertained at the beginning of the Session, 'that without an accommodation w! G. B. Congress ought to declare War before adjourning.' " The Secretary conceded

> That war measures had progressed tardily in Congress & also in the Executive branch, a circumstance inseparable from our System. A period now arrives when some decisive System ought to be taken—an Embargo not exceeding 60 days as prepatory to War has been spoken of without war[.] [P]ublic expections w^d be defeated and our Character destroyed abroad. . . . *[N]o immediate declaration of War being contemplated*, an Embargo of 60 days within which time the Hornet must return, will have the ultimate policy of the Gov! in our hands. . . . The Executive w^d be very glad to know the sentiments of Congress on the Embargo [emphasis in original].

When Harper asked if the executive branch would recommend the embargo by special message, Monroe answered, "If you give me the necessary assurance that it will be acceptable to the House the Executive will recommend it."[23] But later in the meeting Monroe said that the president had some "constitutional Scruples" about recommending an embargo. To this Smilie replied that the "last Embargo" had come from the Executive. The committee then voted to have the chairman prepare an embargo bill, and Monroe stated that "he would inform the President of what had passed & wait upon the Com. again tomorrow & let them know the Opinion of the Executive." On April 1, Madison sent his embargo request to the Congress.[24]

These documents may be interpreted in several ways. Those historians who see a strong executive directing the course of Congress have their hero in Monroe, just as those who feel the president lagged behind the Congress or hid behind "constitutional Scruples" have support for their position.[25] What seems clearest from these documents, however, is the broad nature of the cooperation between the executive and legislative branches during the war session. Monroe acted primarily as a liaison between Congress and President James Madison. Moreover, when the period of time for locating the origins of the war decision is widened to include the Eleventh Congress, Madison qualifies as a leader under the leadership theory employed in this study. Beginning in 1810, Madison fashioned policies which strengthened Republican cohesion and designated the secretary of state as the main communicator between the administration and Congress.

Prior to the second session of the Eleventh Congress, Madison was as perplexed as the House over the best path to follow between war and submission to the belligerents' edicts. Writing to William Pinkney at the beginning of the second session, Madison reported that "the diversity of opinions and prolixity of discussion [make clear that] few are desirous of war; and few are reconciled to submission; yet the frustration of intermediate courses seems to have left scarce an escape from that dilemma."[26] In an attempt to create a position around which all Republicans could unite, Madison proposed what came to be known as Macon's Bills.[27] These bills, opening American trade to whichever country rescinded its edicts, were not to be panaceas for the nation's foreign policy woes; rather, they originated, in Madison's words, "in the difficulty of finding measures that would prevent what Congress had solemnly protested agst., towit, a compleat submission to the Belligerent Edicts. . . . [T]he measure was considered as better than nothing, which seemed to be the alternative, and as part of whatever else might in the progress of the business be found attainable."[28]

Most Republicans did rally behind Macon's Bill #2 (Table 2.4),[29] and Madison's message of January 3, 1811, on East Florida led many Republican congressmen to applaud what they saw as an energetic spirit in the president. Henry Clay, at this time preparing to jump from the lethargic Senate to the more vigorous House, was especially impressed by Madison's message and wrote to a friend, "Upon the whole, the political atmosphere is much more agreeable . . . than it was last year. The President has certainly manifested proper energy in relation to Florida, and if we look abroad we shall find less embarrassments than attended our foreign affairs last winter."[30]

Federalists also noted the change in the president's attitude. According to New Yorker Herman Knickerbocker, the House did not even debate the president's Florida message (no debates are re-corded in the *Annals*). "On Thursday," he wrote to a friend, "we received a Message from the Palace of a confidential nature. The Galleries were cleared and the doors closed[.][T]he remainder of the Day was spent in secret conclave[.] On Saturday this was repeated[.] [T]hus you see that dum Legislation has become the order of the Day at this place." Massachusetts Representative Abijah Bigelow reported that it little benefited the minority party to debate the mea-sures of the third session since "the best speech in the world avails but little with the demo's"; and Bigelow's associate, Samuel Taggart, put it even more bluntly: "speaking has no more effect upon the House than water poured upon a rock."[31]

Madison's move to improve communication with the House came late in the third session with the decision to replace Robert Smith with Monroe. In a public memorandum he prepared to justify his actions, Madison stressed Smith's disruptive influence in the gov-ernment councils. "It had long been felt, and had at length become notorious," Madison wrote, "that the Administration of the Execu-tive Department laboured under a want of harmony & unity, which were equally essential to its energy and its success." Smith, through "language and conduct out of doors," had counteracted "what had been understood within to be the course of the administration and the interest of the public." Thus, Madison wanted someone as secre-tary of state who could work with Congress.

Madison's memorandum on Smith reveals another side of the president's "constitutional Scruples":

> I remarked that where the intention was honest & the object useful, the conveniency of facilitating business in that way was so obvious that it had been practised under every past administration, & w^d be so under every future one; that Executive experience w^d frequently furnish hints & lights for the Legislature; that nothing was more common than for members of Cong^s to apply for them; and that in fact, *such communica-tions, in cases not calling for formal messages, were indispensable to the advantageous conduct of public business.* A resort to formal messages on every occasion where executive information might be useful, was liable to obvious objections [emphasis added].[32]

In other words, Madison felt no reluctance to lead Congress when-ever necessary. He preferred not to send frequent personal direc-tions to the Congress, but the minutes of the Foreign Relations

Committee clearly indicate that Madison effectively used Monroe to communicate indirectly with Congress.

Ironically, some antiwar Republicans, such as John Taylor of Caroline, supported Monroe's appointment because they felt the new Secretary would end the British impasse short of war. Monroe, however, completely shared the Republican consensus that war would follow the failure of commercial restriction. Writing to Taylor immediately prior to the declaration of war, Monroe said that he had done everything in his power to accomplish a peaceful settlement of differences and that he was convinced he had failed because of the refusal of "the present Ministry of England" to accept nothing short of unconditional submission. "This was the plan of the administration in December last," he wrote. "The President's Message announced it; and every step taken by the administration since has led to it." During the session, the executive branch had consulted closely with the committees on foreign relations in both houses, which were "apparently united, and seriously so, as most of the members were, in resisting the foreign aggressions." Thus, Monroe continued, after raising troops, levying taxes necessary for war,[33] and instituting an embargo to protect American shipping from capture once the war began, the administration now asked the Congress to declare war: "the only possible means of giving effect to the just claims of the country on foreign powers."[34]

Monroe's letter aptly summarizes the extent of the cooperation between the legislative and executive branches during the war session. For Republicans, the war decision had always been basically a problem of timing. Some demanded war in 1807 during the *Chesapeake* affair; others, following the Erskine disavowal and the failure of nonintercourse. The final decision for war may have been made as late as the convening of Congress in early November, when the broad outlines of the agreement were fashioned by House and administration leaders. At the same time, internal dissension within the Republican party also forced Madison to take a stronger hand in the party's affairs, and by successfully facilitating discussions between the Congress and his cabinet to produce a declaration of war, Madison qualifies as an effective leader.[35]

It would be a mistake, however, to conclude from this analysis of leadership effectiveness that Madison's role in the events leading to the war declaration made 1812 "Mr. Madison's War." This view,

advanced four decades ago by Abbott Smith, has been revitalized
recently by Rudolph M. Bell.[36] Based upon an analysis of legislative
districts' voting records in the House, Bell argued that the main de-
terminant of the war vote in June of 1812 was Madison's request and
that if prior presidents had requested war, the Congress would have
obliged. What this view neglects, however, and what the leadership
analysis confirms, is the broad consensus within which policy makers worked. Effective leaders are part of the groups they lead, and
the achievement of "certain clearly specified group goals with best
advantage to the individuals comprising the group" provides the
best evidence with which to evaluate leadership effectiveness.[37]

Madison, Monroe, Clay, and the other leaders did not create
this group orientation, however. Without a unity of purpose, manifested in the ability of Republicans to vote together, leadership would
have faltered. The next chapter investigates the partisan voting behavior that formed the second component of the majority party's
movement toward war.

CHAPTER THREE

Model Building

The Partisanship Component

Systematic analysis of roll calls over two decades has demonstrated that the single most determinative variable for a legislator's vote, irrespective of issue or situation, is party affiliation. In the war session, sectional pressures, discussions with colleagues, and individual idiosyncracies influenced congressional voting on selected issues, but overall a legislator's partisan affiliation was the best predictor of his war stance. This is not to say, however, that partisanship became an end in itself for the majority of Republicans in 1812. This chapter investigates how party unity sustained but did not cause the movement toward war.

In order to see the full spectrum of sentiment among Republicans on the main war legislation, one need only look at the troop and tax issues. Both of these issues were direct responses to President Madison's message of November 5, 1811, to the Congress. After appealing that the nation be put into "an armor and an attitude equal to meet the crisis in foreign relations," the president specifically recommended that the military establishment be strengthened and that new sources of revenue be tapped to provide for the expenses of war preparations. On November 29, 1811, New York Republican Peter B. Porter presented to the House the report of a select committee on foreign relations to implement the president's request for additional troops.[1]

As can be seen from Table 3.1, the legislation to raise additional troops gained more support than any other war-related issue in the session, with 76 Republicans in the extremist category. During debate on the troop legislation, supporters of the stronger measures faced two potentially disruptive problems. First, on December 31

Table 3.1[2]
Voting Scales, House Republicans: Twelfth Congress, First Session

Republican	State	Issues						%
		O	Tr	Ta	EW	N	M	
Alston	NC	+	+	+	+	+	+	100
Bassett	Va	+	+	+	+	+	+	100
Blackledge	NC	+	+	+	+	+	+	100
Calhoun	SC	+	+	+	+	+	+	100
Cheves	SC	+	+	+	+	+	+	100
Green	Ma	+	+	+	+	+	+	100
Little	Md	+	+	+	+	+	+	100
Lowndes	SC	+	+	+	+	+	+	100
Dawson	Va	+	+	+	+	+	Ab	100
Winn	SC	+	+	+	+	Ab	Ab	100
Anderson	Pa	+	+	+	+	×	+	83
Bibb	Ga	+	+	+	+	×	+	83
Desha	Ky	+	+	+	+	×	+	83
Grundy	Te	+	+	+	+	×	+	83
Hall, O.	NH	+	+	+	+	×	+	83
King	NC	+	+	+	+	×	+	83
McKee	Ky	+	+	+	+	×	+	83
McKim	Md	+	+	+	+	+	×	83
Newton	Va	+	+	+	+	+	×	83
Ormsby	Ky	+	+	+	+	×	+	83
Pickens	NC	+	+	+	+	×	+	83
Roane	Va	+	+	+	+	×	+	83
Sage	NY	+	+	+	+	×	+	83
Seaver	Ma	+	+	+	+	×	+	83
Smilie	Pa	+	+	+	+	×	+	83
Strong	Vt	+	+	+	+	×	+	83
Turner	Ma	+	+	+	+	+	×	83
Widgery	Ma	+	+	+	+	+	×	83
Wright	Md	+	+	×	+	+	+	83
Brown	Pa	+	+	+	+	×	Ab	80
Harper	NH	+	+	+	+	×	Ab	80
Johnson	Ky	+	+	+	+	×	Ab	80
Morgan	NJ	+	+	+	+	×	Ab	80
New	Ky	+	+	+	+	×	Ab	80
Pleasants	Va	+	Ab	+	+	+	×	80
Ringgold	Md	+	+	Ab	×	+	+	80
Shaw	Vt	+	+	Ab	+	×	+	80

Table 3.1 (*continued*)

Republican	State	\ Issues \ 0	Tr	Ta	EW	N	M	%
Clay, M.	Va	+	+	×	Ab	Ab	+	75
Hyneman	Pa	+	+	Ab	+	×	Ab	75
Taliaferro	Va	+	+	Ab	+	×	Ab	75
Bard	Pa	+	+	+	+	×	×	67
Burwell	Va	+	+	+	+	×	×	67
Butler	SC	+	+	+	+	×	×	67
Cochran	NC	+	+	×	+	×	+	67
Condict	NJ	+	+	+	×	+	×	67
Crawford	Pa	+	+	×	+	×	+	67
Davis	Pa	+	+	+	+	×	×	67
Dinsmoor	NH	+	+	×	+	×	+	67
Earle	SC	+	+	+	+	×	×	67
Findley	Pa	+	+	+	+	×	×	67
Gholson	Va	+	+	+	+	×	×	67
Hall, B.	Ga	+	×	+	+	×	+	67
Kent	Md	+	+	+	×	×	+	67
Lacock	Pa	+	+	+	+	×	×	67
Lefever	Pa	+	+	×	+	×	+	67
Lyle	Pa	+	+	+	+	×	×	67
McCoy	Va	+	+	+	+	×	×	67
Metcalf	NY	+	+	+	×	×	+	67
Moore	SC	+	+	+	×	×	+	67
Pond	NY	+	+	×	+	+	×	67
Roberts	Pa	+	+	+	+	×	×	67
Sevier	Te	+	+	+	+	×	×	67
Smith, J.	Va	+	+	×	×	+	+	67
Troup	Ga	+	+	+	+	×	×	67
Goodwyn	Va	+	Ab	+	+	×	×	60
Richardson	Ma	+	Ab	×	×	+	+	60
Fisk	Vt	+	×	×	+	×	+	50
Hawes	Va	+	+	+	×	×	×	50
Hufty	NJ	×	+	+	×	×	+	50
Nelson	Va	+	×	+	×	+	×	50
Piper	Pa	+	+	+	×	×	×	50
Rhea	Te	+	+	×	+	×	×	50
Seybert	Pa	+	+	+	×	×	×	50
Smith, G.	Pa	+	+	+	×	×	×	50
Bacon	Ma	+	×	+	Ab	×	×	40
Maxwell	NJ	×	+	×	×	Ab	+	40

Table 3.1 (*continued*)

Republican	State	Issues						%
		0	Tr	Ta	EW	N	M	
Sammons	NY	×	+	Ab	×	+	×	40
Williams	SC	×	+	Ab	×	+	×	40
Archer	Md	+	×	+	×	×	×	33
Boyd	NJ	×	+	+	×	×	×	33
Newbold	NJ	×	+	+	×	×	×	33
Tracy	NY	×	+	×	×	+	×	33
Porter	NY	×	+	×	Ab	Ab	×	25
Van Cortlandt	NY	×	+	Ab	×	Ab	×	25
Mitchill	NY	×	+	×	×	Ab	×	20
Whitehill	Pa	+	Ab	×	×	×	×	20
Macon	NC	×	×	×	×	×	+	17
Randolph	Va	×	×	×	×	Ab	Ab	0
Rodman	NY	×	×	Ab	×	×	×	0
Stanford	NC	×	×	×	×	×	Ab	0
	totals	75	76	63	59	23	39	

% means percent "extremist"   M means Militia
0 means Overall Scale   N means Navy
Tr means Troops   + means "extremist"
Ta means Taxes   × means "nonextremist"
EW means Embargo and War   Ab means excessive absences

the Senate sent to the House a bill presented by Virginian William B. Giles to authorize the president to increase the regular army by 25,000 rather than by the 10,000 men proposed in the House resolutions. Giles presented his bill in the Senate to embarrass the administration, specifically Treasury Secretary Albert Gallatin, by showing how unprepared the nation was for war, but administration supporters quickly adopted Giles's higher number so as not to threaten Republican unity. Anti-administration Republicans and Federalists in the House hoped that Giles's bill would weaken the war fever there, but House Republican leaders also took the measure in stride. As Speaker Henry Clay put it, "He was one . . . who was prepared . . . to march on in the road of his duty, at all hazards."[3]

The most concerted opposition came not from those who wanted to embarrass the movement to war by accelerating its progress but rather from "Old Republicans" John Randolph and Richard Stanford, who opposed any and all warlike measures. Randolph warned that Republicans had become "as infatuated with standing armies, loans, taxes, navies, and war as ever were the Essex Junto. What Republicanism is this?" Stanford added that he could not in good conscience support a vote that would negate his actions during the French crisis of the late 1790s.[4] Majority Republicans reacted immediately to these arguments. North Carolinian William R. King said that while Randolph and Stanford were refusing to raise an army with Washington at its head in 1798, he was "at that period conning the lessons of childhood." Whether there was cause for war then did not matter to him: "I am consistent; I find my country degraded by insults unrevenged; almost ruined by her efforts to preserve friendship with nations who feel power and forget right; and, although I am opposed to the principle of having large standing armies in our country, yet . . . under these circumstances, I feel justifiable in departing from the general principle." Similarly, South Carolinian David R. Williams said he would not "drivel out this debate by following some gentlemen through their tedious details concerning the relative importance of the debates of 1798; let us come home to the present times."[5]

Tennessean Felix Grundy spoke most directly to the Old Republicans' arguments. The purposes of raising an army in 1798 and in 1811 were different, he stated, and he called upon the Republican members of the House to consider seriously their situation:

My business at present is to address a particular portion of the members of this House—I mean, sir, the Republican members—and although what I am about to say might be deemed impolitic on ordinary subjects of legislation, yet, at this time and on this occasion, it would be criminal to conceal a single thought which might influence their determination. We should now, Mr. Speaker, forget little party animosities, we should mingle minds freely, and, as far as we are able, commune with the understandings of each other; and, the decision once made, let us become one people, and present an undivided front to the enemies of our country. . . . If your minds are resolved on war, you are consistent, you are right, you are still Republicans; but if you are not resolved, pause and reflect, for should this resolution pass, and you then become fainthearted, remember that you have abandoned your old principles, and trod in the paths of your predecessors.

Grundy told his Republican associates that he felt the party stood on the banks of the Rubicon. "One movement more," he said, "the Rubicon is passed, we are in Italy, and we must march to Rome."[6] Clearly, commitment to the party's current goal of protecting the nation's sovereignty by war was more important to Grundy and his colleagues than the consistency of the party's policies toward raising troops.

On the issue of raising taxes to finance the war effort, however, Republican direction faltered. Only 63 Republicans may be labeled as "extremists" (Table 3.1), and during debates on the tax measures more than once it appeared that the program would be lost. As with the troop legislation, the taxes were a direct response by the Republican majority to Madison's opening message. On February 17, 1812, the Chairman of the Ways and Means Committee, Massachusetts Republican Ezekiel Bacon, presented fourteen resolutions to the House to raise the money necessary to carry on a war with Great Britain.[7] On February 25, Bacon asked three things of his colleagues. First, they should recognize that the report was a specific answer to the president's message. Second, they should adopt the financial measures necessary to pay for a war with Great Britain so that the American people would know how much a war would cost even though the taxes would not begin until after the war was declared. Finally, he asked that all men who wished the resolution to pass be governed by a generous spirit. Certain parts of the tax levies would strike at one section harder than another, and if men were to act only in their self-interest, Bacon warned that the taxes would never pass.[8]

It was this final caveat of Bacon's that proved to be the largest obstacle to implementing the tax program. The problem came to a climax during voting on the resolution to impose a tax of ten cents per bushel on domestic salt. Southern and Western congressmen were especially upset over this resolution, which they claimed would hurt their constituents more than citizens of the seaboard states. On February 28, 1812, the resolution failed by a vote of 22 to 96, and a compromise measure which would have taxed imported salt twenty cents per bushel was also defeated 57 to 60.[9]

Connecticut Federalist Benjamin Tallmadge believed that the salt tax had stopped the war movement in its tracks. Writing to a friend, he recounted the disarray produced by the votes of February 28:

As soon as we came to the *internal Taxes Excise* &c, it was manifest that the Patriotism which they (the Democrats) had boasted of so much, was measured very much by self Interest, popularity and such sort of principles. The Debate being confined solely to the *exclusive Republicans*, they began to criminate one another with want of *true patriotism*, & strong Intimations were given that so long as the burden could be laid on Commerce, they were willing to support the war with great Zeal; but as soon as *Salt* was offered as a fit subject for Taxation, & other matters of domestic manufacture for Excise &c, the war fever subsided. Such remarks from their own friends were very grievous to be borne. On the Salt Tax the Phalanx broke, & if we had not adjourned, I fully believe the Excise Duties would have shared the same fate.[10]

On March 2, however, Republican momentum was restored. Virginian Thomas Gholson, Jr., moved that the vote on the salt tax be reconsidered. Gholson explained to his Republican colleagues that he had voted against the tax to show how the tax would work principally against only one section of the country. He said he much preferred that the salt tax be distributed among those articles which were not "indispensable to life." He had changed his mind, however, since "it now seems that, if the article of salt is excluded, the whole system of taxation will be endangered." Before that should happen, Gholson declared himself prepared to "take the whole draught, just as it has been proposed . . . even if it were hemlock," or even vote two dollars per bushel "rather than see the present course of policy frustrated." He called upon all Republicans to act according to similar concerns:

Mr. Speaker, we who form the majority have all the same end in view: the maintenance of the rights, honor, and independence of the country against the lawless aggressions of our enemy. To attain this end, I would take the best means. Rather than be defeated in the accomplishment of it, I would agree to any means not absolutely intolerable. It is therefore that I, on the present occasion, will concede much of my own opinion, in order to harmonize with, and conciliate those with whom I unfortunately disagree on this particular point. Concession and compromise, among those who have the same common object, are often indispensable duties. It is by this sentiment, sir, that I am actuated. We should not dispute among ourselves. It is by union and harmony only that we can serve our constituents. I, for one, will pledge myself that I will furnish no cause of schism amongst our friends.[11]

In the end Republican consensus prevailed even on the disruptive issue of taxes. On March 11, New Hampshire Representative John A. Harper informed Governor William Plumer that the bills would pass. Despite problems implementing the taxes and unpredictable political effects on the majority party's control of the national and state governments, Harper believed that Republicans would approve the tax bills "rather than to hazard a division in the party."[12]

On each of these issues the willingness of Republicans to compromise discordant beliefs and vote together kept the war movement on track. And in the final war votes, party unity is also the best explanation for the voting behavior of the Republican majority, with 59 of the group in the extremist category (Table 3.1). Still, the issue of Republican partisan attachments should not be overemphasized. Partisan affiliation is the best key to explain a legislator's voting behavior on those items that relate most clearly to the prowar program, but it should not be viewed as the *cause* of the war.

Two war-related issues surfaced during the war session that could not be neatly accommodated within the movement to war— legislation to expand the roles of the navy and militia units. On the surface, one might reasonably have expected the naval issue to have fared exactly as did the troops or tax issues as it too was part of the president's initial message to the Congress. Instead, the naval establishment became the most contested issue of the session. South Carolinian Langdon Cheves was the chairman of the committee charged with addressing that part of the president's message dealing with the navy. Cheves's report advised that the naval establishment should be gradually increased "to the size of our desires [and] of our necessities" and that the program should be begun in conjunction with the present war crisis. Accordingly, the report challenged the lawmakers to fit out all vessels worthy of repair, to build additional frigates, and to construct a new naval dock for the construction of the ships.[13]

In contrast to the debates on the issues of troops and taxes, in which partisan appeals and questions of ideological consistency surfaced rather late in the discussion, Cheves addressed both issues at the beginning of his opening speech on January 17, 1812. The Federalist navy of 1798, he said, "was to be employed for improper objects"; it was only part of a scheme to create unnecessary armies and unnecessary loans and taxes. The present navy was to be begun now as an auxiliary to other war preparations designed to protect American property and rights. For Cheves, this was no ordinary legislation because of the Republican party's traditional animosity toward the navy. But he believed that the fate of the party depended upon its ability to abandon old beliefs and increase the size of the navy. "If this infant Naval Establishment be either abandoned or put down," he said, "the party who now form the majority in this House, and in the country, may run the great risk of becoming the minority, not only within these walls, but in the nation."[14]

Cheves's arguments did not win the day, however, as only 23 Republicans may be classified as extremists on the naval issue (Table 3.1). Republican biases against taxes to support a naval establishment and calculations that American land strength could be used with effect against British colonies in America (her weakness) produced the decision to wage war primarily on land rather than on the seas. In other words, in contrast to the troops and tax issues, with regard to strengthening the navy, Republicans were able to remain faithful to older party principles and still not sacrifice their prowar stance.

On January 28, 1812, South Carolinian David R. Williams introduced a motion equally disruptive to Republican unity. Williams's bill would have divided state militias into three classes: 1) men 18 to 21 years, eligible for service only within their state or territory of residence; 2) men 21 to 31, with no limit on their geographic range; and 3) men 31 to 45, with service limited to their own or adjacent states or territories. Also included in the bill were sections that would have provided every free white male with a gun at age 18 for his service in the militia at a cost of $400,000 annually to the nation.[15]

For unknown reasons, the House recorder reported only a summary of the debates on Williams's resolutions, but only 39 Republicans may be identified as extremists on the militia issue (Table 3.1). On both the naval and militia issues, ideological and sectional differences spotlight to an even greater extent the consensus that existed on the major war legislation. Party unity was a strong bond in crucial, but not all, areas.

It is only when the record of war session voting behavior is compared with that of previous Congresses that one is better able to assess the importance of Republican party unity and the vote for war in 1812. Using cluster-bloc analysis and indexes of cohesion, meaningful comparisons are possible among the Madison, Jefferson, and Adams Congresses. Pairwise agreement scores yielded groups of legislators who voted similarly in three regions, and relationships among the blocs in each section were tested. For most Congresses, two distinct blocks of Republicans and Federalists emerged with minimal cross-party voting (Tables 3.2 and 3.3).[16]

The most important conclusion to be drawn from these analyses is that party unity could not of itself have caused a prowar vote since the majority party always had the numbers and the cohesion necessary for a prowar vote. In fact, if party unity alone could have produced a war decision, war should have come during John Adams's

Table 3.2
Cluster-Bloc Sizes across Congresses

President	House, session	Federalists		Republicans			Totals	
		Bloc	Bloc Plus Fringe	Bloc	Bloc Plus Fringe	Bloc Members	Total Membership	Percent in Either Bloc
Adams	5,1	48	51	45	46	93	106	88
	5,2	49	52	45	45	94	106	89
	5,3	49	57	42	43	91	106	90
	6,1	53	55	42	49	95	106	90
Jefferson	6,2	51	52	48	50	99	106	93
	7,1	30	35	54	62	84	106	79
	7,2	28	33	40	58	68	106	64
	8,1	28	32	46	93	74	142	52
	8,2	32	36	57	84	89	142	63
	9,1	23	28	48	93	71	142	50
	9,2	23	47	48	83	71	142	50
	10,1	23	52	52	89	75	142	53
	10,2	40	58	67	84	107	142	75
Madison	11,1	36	55	57	63	93	142	65
	11,2	41	48	50	80	91	142	64
	11,3	44	47	60	71	104	142	73
	12,1 (until war)	34	44	69	83	103	142	72

Table 3.3
Indexes of Cohesion across Congresses

President	House, session	Federalists Mean Cohesion		Republicans Mean Cohesion	
		All Roll Calls	Foreign Affairs Roll Calls	All Roll Calls	Foreign Affairs Roll Calls
Adams	5,1	74	72	68	65
	5,2	75	78	79	84
	5,3	75	72	87	88
	6,1	81	81	79	82
Jefferson	6,2	84	65	86	95
	7,1	85	87	74	65
	7,2	84	86	59	61
	8,1	72	72	53	62
	8,2	86	74	55	39
	9,1	60	63	44	50
	9,2	58	56	41	50
	10,1	57	61	45	50
	10,2	52	63	53	63
Madison	11,1	76	76	72	69
	11,2	84	81	58	60
	11,3	82	90	69	79
	12,1 (until war)	74	76	59	66

administration, when the majority Federalists enjoyed an average cohesion ranging from 72 to 81 on foreign policy roll calls. Even during the second session of the Eighth Congress, when Republican cohesion reached its lowest point in the period (an index of 39), the majority Republican block technically could have sustained a presidential request for war (57 to 32, or 84 to 36 if the fringe members are considered).

There is, however, an important difference in these periods. Before 1812, Republicans were cohesive but not on the question of war. Therefore, this cohesion could have dissipated upon a presidential request for war if it had come before 1812. That the issue was more than simply a matter of cohesion around particular policies or goals is indicated by taking a closer look at the relationship between the two parties during the Adams, Jefferson, and Madison Congresses. Much of the data contained in Tables 3.2 and 3.3 could have been predicted on the basis of the behavior of modern legislative bodies based simply on the numbers of legislators in the majority and minority parties. When political parties are evenly matched (as they were during the Fifth and Sixth Congresses while Adams was president), pressures on the parties are intensified since even the smallest defection can swing the vote. Therefore, cohesion is usually extremely high, especially in the minority party, since attracting a few votes from the majority can mean victory. However, when there is a wide discrepancy in the size of legislative groupings (as in the Jefferson years), the necessity for bloc voting is lessened and cohesion levels for both the majority and minority parties tend to drop (less for the minority than the majority).

In every way, legislative behavior of both parties under Adams and Jefferson and the Federalists under Madison conform to modern theories and practices. What cannot be predicted, however, is the behavior of Republicans in the Twelfth Congress. They should have behaved as they did during the Jefferson years. Instead, they reversed the downward slide begun during Jefferson's terms and attained levels of cohesion in the third session of the Eleventh House and the first session of the Twelfth House (the point made in chapter 2) that on foreign policy issues closely approximate the cohesion of the majority Federalists under Adams (Table 3.2). The party unity of the war session, therefore, should be taken as a sign that the 1812 situation *was* unique compared to 1798 or 1808, when partisan behavior masked real differences of opinion among members of the majority party.

What all of this means, in summary, is that partisanship does explain the voting behavior of Republicans leading to the war decision, but it cannot explain why Republican legislators perceived certain issues to be related (taxes, troops, embargo, and war) when others (navy and militia) were not. Just as the leadership of Madison, Monroe, Clay, and congressional committees was a crucial component of the movement toward war but cannot be seen as the cause of the war, so partisanship by itself is a dead end in explaining why the war decision came only in 1812 and took the form that it did. Partisanship provided the context within which prowar goals could emerge. Then, group-oriented leaders used partisanship to implement those goals and to preserve group identity and purpose. But even this development does not explain fully how partisanship and leadership helped to produce the war decision.

It is only when a third component, the sophistication of prowar rhetoric in 1812, is considered that one is able to place leadership and partisanship in a proper relationship to the war declaration. What also distinguishes the 1812 situation from previous war situations is the way in which Republicans developed a publicly accountable rationale for war.

CHAPTER FOUR

Model Building

Rhetoric as a Component

By focusing on the leadership and partisanship of decision makers, we have determined that much of the process leading to
war in 1812 was a function of cooperation between the executive and
legislative branches of the government facilitated by the cohesive-
ness of majority-party voting. Madison, acting as a group-oriented
leader through the agency of Secretary of State Monroe, worked
closely with the Republican members of the House Committee on
Foreign Relations to frame the major war legislation of the session
and to provide informal assurances of his administration's support
at crucial points along the way. The product of this coordinated
effort was a consensus among party leaders over the main war legislation sent to Congress. In turn, passage of the bulk of the recommended measures was assured largely by the party loyalties of the
Republican majority. Yet, by itself, this interaction of leadership
with partisanship provides an insufficient account of congressional
behavior, for it leaves unexplained the critical part of the decision-
making process wherein Republicans developed their justification
for calling the nation to arms.

As a third factor, the rhetoric of the majority party facilitated
progress toward a final confrontation with Great Britain by establishing a rationale for war which met standards of public accountability. Republicans could plan on mustering the energies of a disparate people only by drawing upon nationally-shared images, or
what C. Wright Mills has called "vocabularies of motives."[1] Once
identified with the language of legitimate motives, belligerence
could be expected to receive the sanction of the community and the
endorsement of decision makers, for these were national images
shared by the powerful as well as the ordinary members of the pol-

ity.[2] Any Republicans who privately deviated from the national code had to relate to it publicly or risk the rejection of their proposals. They had to take into account national images, rather than simply "objective" facts or strictly partisan goals, when they determined whether war was warranted.[3] In short, policy making was a strategic refraction of reality, or symbolic enactment of perceptual realities, rooted in the nation's vocabulary of acceptable motives.[4] By 1812, Republicans had met the criterion of public accountability by articulating a thoroughly universal appeal for war based on the central proposition that Great Britain was determined to recolonize its commercial rival. A close examination of this theme of recolonization reveals how the most vital symbols of national danger were drawn upon to construct a case for war.

For a systematic study of Republican rhetoric in the Twelfth Congress it is useful to begin by identifying recurrent themes and theme combinations in the addresses of majority party speakers of the House. These themes can be grouped for the purpose of systematic analysis into two sets with three general categories in each (Table 4.1).[5] The first set of themes contributed to the establishment of the intrinsic harmfulness of the situation faced by the nation. It included a category, referred to as "identification of damages," which involved complaints about depredations of the nation's commerce, mistreatment of seamen, incitement of Indians, and other particulars. The next category within the set, called the "lawlessness of conduct" themes, encompassed various charges that the hostile actions of the adversary were in violation of treaties and the law of nations. The final category consisted of "universalization of effects" themes, in which speakers identified the national interests involved in particular incidents. Enumerated items included complaints of commercial privations, agricultural losses, violations of national rights, insults to the nation, threats against independence, and other consequences of the enemy's transgressions.

The second set of themes reflected the efforts of speakers to prove that hostile actions and harmful effects were intentional. The first group, "negation of justifications," included repudiations of the enemy's negotiation tactics, refutations of the claim that the enemy was acting only in self-defense, and other themes that contested various justifications for the enemy's hostile conduct. A second group-

Table 4.1
War Justification Themes for the Early Republic War Rhetoric

I. Establishment of Harms
    A. Identification of Damages (specification of the enemy's action against the United
        States)
        1. Depredations on Commerce
            a. attacks on and/or captures of ships
            b. confiscations of cargoes and/or ships
            c. blockades, Orders in Council, Decrees
        2. Mistreatment of Seamen
            a. impressments
            b. imprisonments
            c. physical injury and/or death
        3. Attacks on U.S. Warships
        4. Violations of Territorial Integrity
            a. blockades of U.S. ports and harbors
        5. Incitement of Indians
        6. Generalized References to Damages Inflicted, Attacks, Aggressions
        7. Conspiracy Against U.S. Government
    B. Lawlessness of Conduct
        1. Violations of Treaties
        2. Violations of the Law of Nations, of Belligerents' Rights
        3. Violations of Moral Law
        4. General References to Lawlessness
    C. Universalization of Effects (the effects of the adversary's actions on the victim)
        1. Effects on Commercial Interests
            a. effects on commercial states and/or citizens
            b. effects on the availability of seamen
            c. effects on commerce in general
        2. Effects on Agriculture, Agricultural States, and/or Citizens
        3. Effects on Other Specific Segments of the Economy
        4. Threats to National Unity/Secession
        5. Violations of National Rights
            a. neutral rights
            b. commercial rights
            c. territorial rights
        6. Violations of Citizens' Rights to Protection, to Protection of Their Property, and
            to Protection of Their Commerce
        7. Insults to the National Honor/Character, Humiliations, Degradation
        8. Submission/Threats to the Nation's Independence (sovereignty), Surrender
            of Rights
        9. Generalized References to Negative Effects on the Nation
            a. generalized references to economic effects and others
            b. the safety of the nation

Table 4.1 (*continued*)

        c.   generalized references to injuries suffered
        d.   harms to the national interests
    10. Generalized References to Injustice/Wrongs
II. Determination of Hostile Intentions
    A. Negation of Justifications for the Adversary's Conduct
        1. Refusal to Negotiate
        2. Repudiation of the Retaliation/Self-Defense Excuses
        3. Rebuttal of Claims to Legality of the Adversary's Restrictive Policies
        4. References to America's Innocence/Efforts to Secure Peace/Forebearance/ Love of Peace
        5. General Rejections of Justifications for the Adversary's Conduct
    B. Denigration of the Adversary's Character
        1. Arrogance/Pride
        2. Tyranny/Oppressiveness
        3. Robbery/Piracy
        4. Avarice (for commerce)
        5. Jealousy
        6. Lust for Power/Ambition
        7. Insincerity/Dishonesty/Deception/Perfidy
        8. General Denigration
    C. Imputation of Hostile Intentions
        1. Destruction of a Commercial Rival/Maritime Supremacy
        2. Plans of Domination (in general)
        3. Destruction of the U.S.'s Independence/Usurpation of its Freedom/Reduction to a Colonial State
        4. General References to Hostility toward the U.S.
        5. Forcing U.S. to Fight the Adversary's Enemy
        6. Plans to Attack the U.S.
        7. Destruction of U.S. Commerce

ing within this same set, the "denigration of character" themes, involved slurs that associated the enemy with negative qualities consistent with hostile intentions. These characterizations included "arrogance," "avarice," and "lust for power." Finally, there was the direct "imputation of hostile intentions" category, charges which ranged from general references of hostility toward the United States to the claim that the enemy would not be satisfied until America had been recolonized.

To determine the relative importance of these several themes, a sample of majority party speakers was selected, and their major addresses on war-related issues were subjected to a line-by-line analysis of thematic content. The sample included six speakers and two additional reports from the House Committee on Foreign Relations, comprising a total of 3,524 lines of discourse.[6] From these data, it was possible to develop an index of thematic densities (a proportional measure of the frequency of occurrence of each theme) by calculating the proportion of lines utilized by a theme, based on the total number of lines in a given document or set of documents. A summary of results for the Twelfth Congress is provided in Table 4.2. A high figure, such as .117, indicates a heavy thematic density and therefore a frequent appearance of the theme, i.e., it appears in almost twelve percent of the lines in the sample of speeches. Con-

Table 4.2
Thematic Densities (Proportions of Occurrence):
Twelfth House, First Session

Themes	Densities	Themes	Densities
IA 1	.117	IIA 1	.025
2	.038	2	.064
3	.001	3	.022
4	.007	4	.051
5	.059	5	.001
6	.015	Subtotal	.163
7	.005		
Subtotal	.242	B 1	.003
		2	.004
B 1	.001	3	.003
2	.026	4	.004
3	.001	5	.007
4	.006	6	.001
Subtotal	.034	7	.010
		8	.019
C 1	.047	Subtotal	.051
2	.024		
3	.001	C 1	.016
4		2	.001
5	.080	3	.003
6	.012	4	.004
7	.048	5	.006
8	.110	6	
9	.037	7	
10	.027	Subtotal	.030
Subtotal	.386		
		Total	.906

versely, a low figure, such as .001, indicates low density, or infrequent appearance of the theme.

The principal themes of speakers in the Twelfth Congress included depredations of commerce (IA1), incitement of Indians (IA5), several attempts to universalize the effects of the British actions on Americans (IC1, IC5, IC7, and IC8), repudiation of self-defense excuses (IIA2), and references to American innocence (IIA4). Additionally, attention was given to the mistreatment of seamen (IA2), to the negative effects on the nation from British policies (IC9), and to the generalized denigration of the enemy's character (IIB8 and IIB7). Speakers expressed concern over violations of the law of nations, harms to agricultural interests, injustices and wrongs to the nation, British refusal to negotiate, the illegality of restrictive policies, and attempts to destroy a commercial rival (IB2, IC2, IC10, IIA1, IIA3, and IIC1). It is of particular note that the perceived effects on commercial interests (IC1) were not singled out so much as damages to the rights and independence of the nation (IC5 and IC8) were stressed.

Comparing the patterns of association between the themes listed reveals even more clearly the fundamental structure of Republican prowar rhetoric in 1812. To determine which themes were linked with one another, a count was made of the number of lines in which each one of the most emphasized themes appeared together with other themes. Those which appeared together in at least 10 percent of the lines in which they were mentioned were considered to be "associated." This rather conservative criterion produced the set of primary associations recorded in Table 4.3 (see also Table 4.4).[7]

The tendency of Republican speakers to universalize the threat to the nation is apparent in the ways they chose to associate themes. Attacks on commerce (IA1) were not even connected with the theme of harm to commercial interests (IC1). Instead, an effort was made to broaden the concern over commercial interests (IC1) by associating it with the welfare of agricultural interests (IC2). In addition, the theme of attacks on commerce (IA1) was not directly linked to the question of sovereignty (IC8), but, rather, indirectly through their mutual association with the theme of national rights (IC5). National honor (IC7) was also discussed in terms of national rights (IC5) and independence (IC8). Furthermore, the theme of British attacks on U.S. commerce (IA1) was very closely linked to efforts by Republi-

Table 4.3
Association of Themes: Twelfth House, First Session

IA1<	>	IC5
	<	>IIA2
IA5		>IIB8
IC1	>	IC2
IC5	>	IC8
IC7	>	IC5
	<	> IC8
		> IC9
IC10	>	IA1
		> IC5
		> IC7
IIA3	>	IB2
		>IC10
IIA4	>	IA1

(>)   Indicates that the association was established at .10
        in only one direction, i.e., the theme on the left of the
        sign was linked to the theme on the right of the sign
        at least 10 percent of the time but not vice versa.

(< >) Indicates that the association was established at .10
        in both directions.

can speakers to refute those excuses of retaliation and self-defense (IIA2) that had been offered by opposition spokesmen as explanations of England's hostile policies. Overall, attacks on commerce were not connected to narrow material interests but associated instead with national rights, while national rights were associated with honor and honor with sovereignty.

Others previously have observed this emphasis on national honor, rights, and independence in the war rhetoric of 1812. According to Norman K. Risjord, there had been a "gradual conversion of the average Republican from Jeffersonian pacifism to a vigorous defense of America's neutral rights [stemming in large part from] a growing realization that the only alternative to war was submission and national disgrace."[8] James R. Andrews adds that the defense of the nation's rights to prosperity had become "a question of national honor."[9] And as Larry James Winn concludes, regarding the main themes of the War Hawks, "The United States had to assert and protect its rights if it were to deserve the title 'independent nation.' Terms like 'liberty,' 'rights,' 'honor,' 'patriotism,' and 'freedom' per-

Table 4.4
Mean Proportions for Association of Themes in 1812

	IA1	IA2	IA5	IC1	IC5	IC7	IC8	IC10	IIA2	IIA3	IIA4	IIC1
IA1												
A2	.088	.090	.088	.066	.209	.037	.060	.107	.278	.061	.130	
A3					.032	.062	.044	.025			.042	
A4	.030		.020		.004	.025	.025					
A5	.005				.004	.012	.014				.004	
A6	.005	.062	.007		.032	.012		.060			.039	.035
A7		.005										
B1					.011					.204		
B2	.050				.074			.012	.041			
B3												
B4	.005	.014	.007		.004			.024	.018		.028	.018
C1	.033	.005			.032	.025	.011					
C2	.018			.144	.011	.019	.025					
C3				.039			.016					
C4												
C5	.105	.043	.007	.050	.004	.118	.090	.119	.071	.061	.063	.018
C6	.005	.052			.071	.044	.160		.006			.035
C7	.035	.047	.014	.017	.117	.280		.143	.030		.021	
C8	.055	.076	.034	.050	.025	.360	.008	.083	.065		.025	
C9	.013	.010		.006	.032	.075	.016	.083			.021	
C10	.028	.010			.039	.012		.012		.163	.018	
IIA1	.025				.035	.031	.030	.048	.012		.011	
A2	.163				.011			.024				
A3	.008							.095				

	N=399	N=211	N=148	N=181	N=283	N=161	N=368	N=84	N=169	N=49	N=284	N=57
A4	.090				.067	.050	.025				.004	
A5		.057										
B1	.013				.018	.012	.005	.048	.012			
B2	.005		.007		.014	.012		.024				
B3	.005						.008	.012	.018		.011	
B4	.035	.014			.050	.019	.005		.012			.053
B5								.060				
B6						.019					.011	
B7											.007	
B8	.005	.024	.243		.004	.025		.048			.039	
C1				.006								
C2	.003					.012	.035					
C3			.020		.007		.008					
C4	.008				.007						.007	.018
C5	.018				.007						.004	

vaded the rhetoric of the War Hawks as they appealed to the national pride of their countrymen."[10]

These earlier studies, however, have overlooked a fundamental characteristic of the prowar rhetoric which deepened the significance of the frequent appeals to national honor, rights, and sovereignty. In addition to their efforts to refute the excuses that had been offered for Britain's hostile conduct toward the United States, Republican spokesmen in the Twelfth Congress charged that Great Britain actually planned to destroy America as a commercial rival and that the several violations of America's rights over the past number of years were ample evidence of those evil designs. In the words of the House Committee on Foreign Relations, "When all these circumstances are taken into consideration, it is impossible for your committee to doubt the motives which have governed the British Ministry in all its measures towards the United States since the year 1805. Equally it is impossible to doubt, longer, the course which the United States ought to pursue towards Great Britain."[11] Other speakers put it more colorfully and directly: the British government "sickens at our prosperity" and was again "endeavoring to reduce us" to a "colonial state" because of a desire for "maritime supremacy" and "jealousy" over the anticipated "maritime greatness of this Republic."[12]

Dismissing alternative explanations for continued British harassments, Republican orators pushed the recolonization motive to the forefront as they systematically treated continued attacks on commerce and other acts of hostility as signs of British designs to reestablish a maritime hegemony by subjugating a commercial rival. When this connection was made between continued commercial depredations and hostile intentions to recolonize the nation, Republicans had articulated a truly national cause for which the country as a whole could be asked to fight. In the words of New Hampshire Congressman John A. Harper, Great Britain's conduct "bespeaks a determination to rule us, and can only be answered by the appeal to the God of Battles."[13] At the heart of the issue was not simply that there existed an accumulation of wrongs, nor that any one of those wrongs in itself warranted a declaration of war, but that a consistent pattern had emerged with the clear implication that any continuation of peaceful policies and diplomacy would only play into the hands of an antagonist who had both motive and opportunity to usurp the nation's freedom and deprive its citizens of the principal advantages of their revolution.[14]

The theme of recolonization enabled Republicans to nationalize the appeal for war by focusing attention on some of the most compelling vocabularies of motives available to those who would call a nation to arms, i.e., those related to the evil intentions of the adversary. As Perelman and Olbrechts-Tyteca have pointed out, any phenomenon (in this case, British depredations of American commerce) can be endowed with greater significance and a sense of permanence by considering it as a reflection of an agent's (in this case, Great Britain's) intentions. The motives which determine an agent's actions will be considered as "the reality hidden behind the purely external manifestations." It is chiefly by establishing correspondences between an agent's various acts that one establishes belief in "the existence of the alleged intention."[15] Thus, Republicans were better able to substantiate the threat to the nation's independence by emphasizing British motives over British actions through rhetorical tactics that linked the several particular transgressions to one another as so many external manifestations of a diabolical enemy's abiding hostility toward the Republic. By emphasizing Britain's diabolism, Republicans drew upon basic national images for unifying public opinion against an external enemy as well as for influencing those charged with the responsibility to act in the nation's defense.[16]

The significance of this strategy of diabolism, for substantiating the theme of recolonization and thereby nationalizing the call to arms, is such that a closer examination of the rhetoric of those who advanced it allows for greater insight into an important aspect of the process leading to war. Republicans, that is, did more than simply assert that the sovereignty and independence of the United States were being deliberately and systematically violated by Great Britain.[17] They also devised a number of tactics to dramatize the image of British intransigence and the threat of subjugation, tactics which in one way or another served to link the record of British depredations to a set of criteria for judging hostile intentions.

When Madison greeted the new Congress in November of 1811, his annual message charged it with "putting the United States into an armor and an attitude demanded by the crisis." A call to prepare the nation for war was necessary, the president suggested, because "the British Cabinet perseveres" in its abuse of the nation's lawful commerce, notwithstanding America's protracted moderation and offers of reconciliation. This was "evidence of hostile inflexibility" with intent of "trampling on rights which no independent nation can relinquish."[18] With this statement, Madison set forth the function of prowar rhetoric (i.e., to put the nation into an attitude demanded by the crisis) and foreshadowed the forms of discourse with which the task would be completed. By emphasizing the criterion of perseverance and projecting images of force on the part of Great Britain, Madison and the majority party orators focused attention on an enemy's "hostile inflexibility." Responding to the president's charge, Republicans advanced a singular image of Britain's fixed and determined hostility toward American independence by means of a narrative account, the logic, arrangement, and style of which portrayed an adversary who had initiated and persisted in frequent and diverse hostilities toward the United States over an extended period of time.

The first of these criteria of hostile intentions emerged as the claim that America had been unexpectedly and violently assailed by Great Britain, i.e., through no initiation of its own, the nation was victimized by a "cool, deliberate, intentional indignity."[19] This indictment of the enemy by its very vagueness could refer to any or all of a number of blockades, impressments, diplomatic reversals, ship seizures or other maritime aggravations while ignoring the renewal of the Napoleonic wars and thereby discounting an obvious alternative explanation for British conduct. The frequency and diversity of, by then, familiar abuses were also communicated through abstract references to "the lawless aggressions of Great Britain" and various protests over "so many acts of violence and oppression."[20] And as the House Committee on Foreign Relations systematically reviewed "the multiplied wrongs of the British Government since the commencement of the present war" between France and England, its report added a sense of timelessness to the enemy's transgressions— as if there would be no end to Britain's plundering of the former colonies.[21] Most notably, though, the committee observed that the enemy "perseveres in these aggressions" in spite of American remonstrances and that it must therefore be concluded that the nation's sovereignty and independence were being "deliberately and systematically violated."[22]

British persistence, that is, was the decisive criterion by which

Republicans justified their inference of fixed and hostile intentions, and the most significant of their rhetorical tactics were those that tended to reinforce images of a relentless march toward American subjugation. Accordingly, the logic of prowar rhetors often took the form of a disjunctive syllogism; either the British were sincere about issuing their Orders in Council for purposes of self-defense, as would have been indicated by a favorable response to Macon's Bill No. 2 following Napoleon's revocation of his Decrees; or they were hostile toward the United States, as had been proven by their unfavorable response to the bill. No middle ground was allowed between an attribution of friendly or hostile motives when speakers "described" a course of events that led to an inevitable conclusion. Samuel McKee presented the argument as follows:

> The law of May, 1810 was enacted with a hope that the terms thereby offered to the belligerents, respectively, would induce the one or the other to accept them, and withdraw their orders or decrees. And an expectation was also entertained, that if one of the parties could be induced to relinquish their orders or decrees, the other party would follow the example; and, if this just expectation should be met by a perseverance of either of the parties in their orders or decrees, after their adversary had accepted the invitation thus given, it would test the sincerity of the various and repeated declarations made by them, respectively, that their orders and decrees, affecting our commerce, were reluctantly issued in their own just defence.[23]

As did others, McKee concluded that the "fixed and determined hostility of one of the parties toward the United States would be (as it certainly now is) most clearly proved."[24] To bolster the key assumption upon which McKee's conclusion rested, Republicans simply turned to the authority of the president's unequivocal declaration of the "successive confirmations of the extinction of the French decrees."[25] In this fashion, they managed to present at least the form of a logical case for translating British persistence into a significant sign of evil and fixed motives.

To underscore the implications of British persistence and convey a sense of urgency about the timing of a war declaration, prowar speakers also utilized a form of climactic arrangement, based upon a spatial and temporal sequencing of events which projected the systematic progression of the enemy's encroachments toward an impending assault on the body politic itself. In its final recommendation for war, the House Committee on Foreign Relations employed this scheme by presenting the various complaints against England in the order, first, of blockades, then Orders in Council, followed by impressment of American seamen, Indian uprisings, and finally the Henry affair involving the British "secret agent" sent to agitate the American citizenry against their government's foreign policy. This ordering of events was not that of a simple chronology, but one which moved progressively and climactically from British policies that were construed as applying to other neutrals as well as to the United States, to actions affecting America more singularly and specifically—first on the seas, then on the nation's borders, and finally within its borders. Even the inference of hostile intentions was stated more strongly with the recounting of each progressive transgression, ending with the statement that "there is no bound to the hostility of the British government towards the United States; no act, however unjustifiable, which it would not commit to accomplish their ruin."[26] Only after all complaints had been mentioned and tied to the inference of hostile designs did the report turn to a refutation of the various explanations offered to vindicate British encroachments, suggesting again by an arrangement of topics that each aggression was, above all else, to be taken as an indicator of the adversary's motives.[27]

Republicans furthered their account of the motives governing England's system of hostile aggression, and reduced ambiguities regarding its purported desire "to destroy a rival," with still another rhetorical device that was perhaps their basic linguistic resource for transforming the observation of persistence into a controlling image of diabolism.[28] Their discourse infused with decivilizing metaphors of force, majority party speakers conjured up long-standing prejudices against the British and interlaced them with the theme of recolonization by grounding the image of the enemy's conduct in a language of power and physical confrontation which led easily to the conclusion that America would inevitably be subjugated by the British brute unless its persistent advance was soon repulsed through a corresponding application of physical force. As they recounted British "depredations," prowar speakers favored metaphorical vehicles such as "trampled," "wrested," "bullied," "kicked," and "pounded" to focus attention on the enemy's known resources and sinister propensities for pursuing maritime power and commercial gain at the expense of other nations and without regard for international law.

Joseph Desha warned against "tamely" watching "our rights wrested from us."[29] According to the House Committee on Foreign Relations and Peter B. Porter, the British had "advanced with bolder and continually increasing strides" to the point where soon they would be "trampling on our persons."[30] Henry Clay, cultivating similar images in his public speeches as well as his private correspondence, argued that Britain was "everywhere pounding us" and claimed to have "complete proof that she will do everything to destroy us."[31] Porter agreed, warning that if the nation "tamely submitted to one cool, deliberate, intentional indignity," it "might safely calculate to be kicked and cuffed for the whole of the remainder of [its] life."[32] The inexorable march of Britain's monstrous force, Republicans reasoned, could lead only to national subjugation unless war was declared. As Jefferson summed up the situation in a letter to William Duane on April 20, 1812, "We are then, it seems, to have no intermission of wrongs from England but at the point of the bayonet. We have done our duty of exhausting all the peaceable means of obtaining justice, and must now leave the issue to the arbitration of force."[33]

Four months previous to Jefferson's letter, Joseph Desha remarked that the nation had been "buffeted," "kicked," and "bullied" by Great Britain to the point where he could discover only "a manifest disposition to persist in her lawless aggressions."[34] Throughout the war session, in fact, Republicans extended this essential image of British brutality to its logical conclusion which, according to Jonathan Roberts, would be "absolute recolonization."[35] Arguing that war should never be resorted to except when it is clearly justified by the most urgent and necessary causes, Calhoun confidently concluded that the "extent, duration, and character of the injuries received; the failure of those peaceful means heretofore resorted to for the redress of our wrongs" proved that war was necessary. "The evil still grows," he continued, "and in each succeeding year swells in extent and pretension beyond the preceding." The criteria for establishing evil intentions had been applied, and the verdict was forthcoming: the United States must resist "the colonial state to which again that Power is endeavoring to reduce us."[36] As one citizen wrote to Jonathan Roberts, the enemy was a "*Jackal* who panders to his insatiable appetite."[37] Roberts obviously concurred when he wrote that Britain's "lawless spirit of plunder" had made it a common feeling among Republicans that aggression could no longer be born without resistance, for the alternative was "colonial vassalage."[38]

Referring in his private correspondence to the Henry plot, "devised by the British . . . for the dismemberment of the U. States," Thomas Gholson displayed an intuitive sense of the importance of Republican war rhetoric and the image of diabolism in particular. "This profligate and outrageous conduct of the British government," he wrote, "it is hoped will unite all honest Americans in the defence of our violated rights."[39] As Republicans mustered the resources of logic, arrangement, and metaphor to highlight an image of English malevolence, opponents of the war insisted upon a far more practical and materialistic definition of the situation.[40] Federalists, that is, together with the few dissidents from the majority party, emphasized that the United States had much to lose and little to gain from a war with Great Britain. Daniel Sheffey argued that he was "fully sensible of the indignities offered to us, and the repeated violations of our rights as a neutral nation." But, he added, "this is not enough for me. I must be persuaded that there is a rational hope that war will remedy the evil which we experience, and that it will not bring with it others much more to be dreaded than that under which we labor."[41] Others pointed out how unprepared the country was to fight one of the two greatest military powers on earth, stressing that current circumstances undermined the old European balance of power which previously had protected the rights of weak neutrals. Americans, they argued, must adapt to new realities rather than delude themselves into exercising "any right to the full extent of its abstract nature." The government should avoid "pretensions, right in theory [but] urged without due consideration of our relative power."[42]

From an economic standpoint as well, opponents contended, war was unreasonable and unnecessary. All that the Republican majority would accomplish was "to enrich the commissaries and contractors from Michillimackinac to Niagara and Frontignac." With an eye toward Canada, John Randolph complained, misguided gentlemen advocated "a war not of defence, but of conquest, of aggrandizement, of ambition; a war foreign to the interest of this country."[43] Federalists argued that, even considering the Orders in Council, the opportunities for commerce were still rich and extensive.[44] Since, as Sheffey suggested, "this nation's honor is the prosperity and happiness of the people," there was little to recommend a call to arms.[45] Peace was by far "the policy which most comported with the character, condition, and interest of the United States."[46]

Peace, which to majority party Republicans was another word for submission, promised the nation no such advantages, according to the proponents of war. Henry Clay, among others, maintained that if "pecuniary considerations alone were to govern there is sufficient motive for war."[47] But matters of profit and loss were neither the sole nor most important consideration. Their significance came from association with the issue of Great Britain's challenge to the young republic's survival. Whether defense cost more than it profited the nation, Calhoun emphasized, a timid and calculating avarice must never disgrace the seat of sovereignty and blind the nation to the laws of self-preservation.[48]

In fact, the principal function of the Republicans' prowar stance was to keep the perspective focused on the sinister roots of England's conduct and away from its circumstantial causes. Federalists and dissident Republicans, in the meantime, advocated an alternative account of world affairs which de-emphasized human volition as the main source of America's troubles. "The present state of the European world," Sheffey insisted, "is the primary cause from which those principles that have so seriously affected our commerce have received their origin. And to me it appears vain to expect that our neutral rights will be respected, until the causes which have subverted every venerable principle . . . shall no longer exist."[49] Circumstances, not men with evil designs, had caused Britain to impinge upon America's rights. Even the prowar Republicans, claimed their critics, were driven by material considerations rather than abstract principles. They were after the "unmolested commerce to France and her dependencies" and that "rich vein of Gennessee land" to the north, whether they knew it or not.[50] The country must learn to acknowledge and "participate in the evils (in some shape) which have fallen on the community of civilized man."[51] It must submit to the world of conditions rather than flail at illusionary evildoers supposedly out to enslave free peoples.

At the root of the controversy between pro- and antiwar speakers lay essentially different vocabularies of motives. While opponents of the war argued from the premise that impersonal circumstances dictated national policies and international affairs, proponents insisted that culprits and conspirators were responsible for an assault on American independence. Each side talked past the other as it offered the nation alternative interpretations of the same events. John Randolph observed in defeat that the "avenues to the public ear are closed against Truth. . . . It is a hopeless task to address one's self to [Congress]. . . . I do not pretend to argue with [the ruling faction], for I speak a language which they cannot understand."[52] Federalists, who knew they would remain the minority voice at least temporarily, eventually withdrew from the debate after their views had been recorded, resolving to give the governing party ample opportunity to destroy its credibility with the voters. The Republican strategy of diabolism, though, had injected into the dispute over national rights and sovereignty a dramatic sense of the seriousness and urgency of America's predicament. Each of their rhetorical tactics advanced an appeal for action as it reinforced a theme that called up deep-rooted prejudices against Britain as a commercial monopolist.[53] An assertive logic couched in didactic tones promoted efforts to make an unmitigated accusation of hostile intentions sound reasonable, while metaphors of force and the climactic narrative of British depredations characterized the enemy as a brutal and intransigent aggressor. As the citizens of Norristown, Pennsylvania resolved on May 19, 1812, the British government was "an object of detestation [to] the Civilized world" whose "crimes" and "perfidy" were a threat to "the very existence of this Nation as an Independent Republic."[54] Despite the protests of Federalists and minority Republicans, majority party speakers had established what they believed to be the final justification for war by molding basic national images into the vision of a voracious British beast preying upon its victim's liberties.

This analysis of the role played by Republican rhetoric, together with the previous examination of contributions made by leadership and partisanship, provides a more precise understanding of the dynamics of congressional behavior than does a political interpretation of the war that emphasizes such underlying causes as republican ideology. Certainly, ideology and other forces contributed to the general make-up of the situation facing the majority party in 1812, but the actual decision to declare war was the immediate product of key behaviors which interacted upon and reinforced one another in a unique way at that particular moment. More than any other single factor, party loyalty constrained the voting of individuals in Congress. However, just as partisanship thereby facilitated the task of leading the Congress, it neither supplied that leadership nor provided the grounds for justifying group-endorsed policies. The close coordination and group-oriented leadership of Republicans in executive and legislative positions made possible consensus on the specific war legislation to be proposed, while secondarily reinforcing group identity. In order for party leaders to formulate the proposed legislation and for the party to endorse it, there also had to be in place a thoroughly developed justification for war based upon the nation's vocabularies of acceptable motives. With the articulation of what was at least potentially a universally appealing call to save the Republic from the threat of recolonization by a diabolical enemy, members of the majority party were better able to maintain their unity as they voted on the various war measures before them. Ultimately, the rhetorical sophistication of speakers who dramatized the recolonization theme, combined with the propensity of Republicans to vote as a party, readied Congress to respond to the initiatives of the president and legislative leaders and to meet the exigencies of the situation with a declaration of war.

CHAPTER FIVE

The War Crisis of 1798

A Variation on the Madison Years

So far we have suggested that by focusing on three components of the process by which the Congress declared war in 1812—leadership, partisanship, and rhetoric—it is possible to reconstruct the movement toward war. In creating the model, it was useful to make comparisons with the war crises of 1798 and 1807 in order to spotlight the way the components of the model functioned in the 1812 situation. Now that the model has been developed, it is instructive to apply it to the two previous war crises to "test" the model's interpretive value. By studying how leadership, partisanship, and rhetoric functioned in the Adams and Jefferson Congresses, a better assessment can be made of why the Congress did not declare war until 1812.

During debates on the war legislation, the time period most often cited by antiwar speakers as being analogous to 1812 was the Quasi-War period of John Adams's administration. Certainly, these similarities were not lost on Henry Adams, who wrote his monumental *History of the United States During the Administration of Thomas Jefferson and James Madison* in large part to vindicate his great-grandfather's administration.[1] Writing of Madison's imminent retirement in 1816, Henry Adams indirectly pitted Madison, and Jefferson by extension, against Adams:

> Party divisions had so nearly disappeared that nothing prevented the President elect [Monroe] from selecting as the head of his Cabinet the son of the last Federalist President, who had been the object of more violent attack from the Republican party than had been directed against any other Federalist. Old Republicans, like [Nathaniel] Macon and John Randolph, were at a loss to know whether James Monroe or J. Q. Adams had departed farthest from their original starting-points. At

times they charged one, at times the other, with desertion of principle; but on the whole their acts tended to betray a conviction that J. Q. Adams was still a Federalist in essentials, while Monroe had ceased to be an old Republican. In the political situation of 1817, if Jefferson and his contemporaries were right in their estimates, Federalist views of government were tending to prevail over the views of the Jeffersonian party.[2]

In showing how Republicans in power reversed their program in 1798 and how J. Q. Adams was still "Federalist in essentials," Henry Adams was putting his family's best foot forward. The similarities that Henry Adams focuses on, however, with regard to foreign policy alternatives and factionalism between the parties, mask important differences in the situations the two presidents faced. Partisanship, leadership, and rhetoric functioned differently in the two periods.

With regard to the voting behavior of congressmen throughout the Adams administration, partisanship is even more the chief explanation for voting than under Madison. From the first session of the Fifth Congress through the first session of the Sixth Congress, Federalist and Republican blocs were highly cohesive, persistent, and evenly divided across the period (Tables 3.2 and 3.3). This does not conform with Rudolph M. Bell's conclusion that in the 1790s "legislative behavior . . . on foreign policy questions differed substantially from actions on domestic affairs."[3] When cohesion indexes on foreign policy and all roll calls are compared, no important difference in voting by legislators is apparent. Also, Bell isolates ten "factions" in the first session of the Fifth Congress that he traces over the other two sessions.[4] Again, our data do not support Bell's conclusions that party voting came only in the Sixth Congress. The first session of the Fifth Congress was the least partisan of the period and is, therefore, not the most representative of the Adams Congresses. Partisanship was the most common pattern during the period and reached levels as high as or higher than during Madison's presidency.

Would these levels of cohesion have persisted, however, had Adams asked for war? Earlier interpretations support grandson Charles Francis Adams's contention that the president could have gotten a declaration of war but that the war would have been disastrous for the country.[5] More recently, however, scholars have emphasized the role of the Congress—especially the Republican minority—and have concluded that a war declaration would never have passed.[6] More important than the Republican opposition tactics, however, is the fact that the quantitative strength of the Federalist bloc in the second session of the Fifth House—the time when Adams was the closest to war and the session that produced the most warlike legislation of his administration—masks important attitudinal diversities among the majority party members. Two scales of roll calls during the session (one a scale of foreign policy roll calls during the entire session and the other a scale of votes taken after March 17, 1798) indicate that opinions were fairly well distributed among Federalists in all sections of the country (Table 5.1).[7]

This division is even more evident when compared with Republican voting during the war session of the Twelfth Congress. As Table 5.1 indicates, there were far more moderate Federalists in the second session of the Fifth House than moderate Republicans in the war session, when extremist positions predominated in both parties (Table 5.2). Compared with the Republicans of the war session, when 13 percent were either moderates or nonaggressives (11 of 86), Federalists in the second session of the Fifth Congress divided into almost three times as many moderates or nonaggressives (15 of 48, or 31 percent in the foreign policy scale; and 20 of 50, or 40 percent on the important votes following May 17, 1798). Simply put, Federalists under Adams pursued more options than did Republicans under Madison. Differences of opinion regarding convoying merchant vessels and seizing French ships as well as restrictive domestic legislation severely weakened party cohesion. Therefore, the relatively weaker partisan attachments in the Adams Congresses undermine the hypothesis that had John Adams asked for a declaration of war he would have attained it. At best, he faced the prospect of a divided Congress and party.[8]

The leadership situation each president faced also pinpoints the similarities and differences between the Adams and Madison periods. The two groups with which both men worked most closely as president in determining foreign policy were the cabinet and the Congress. Adams "inherited" Washington's cabinet comprised of Timothy Pickering, James McHenry, Oliver Wolcott, Jr., and Charles Lee. Of these, only Lee was loyal to Adams. The other three worked in varying degrees most closely with Alexander Hamilton,

Table 5.1
Summary of Scales for Fifth House, Second Session: Division by Section and Party

	Federalists				Republicans			
	Overall Foreign Policy Scale		Votes After 3/17/98		Overall Foreign Policy Scale		Votes After 3/17/98	
	Number	Percent	Number	Percent	Number	Percent	Number	Percent
Northeast								
Aggressive	17	74	16	67				
Moderate	6	26	8	33	1	50		
Nonaggressive					1	50	2	100
Subtotals	23	100	24	100	2	100	2	100
Middle								
Aggressive	14	70	13	65	3	27	4	36
Moderate	6	30	7	35				
Nonaggressive					8	73	7	64
Subtotals	20	100	20	100	11	100	11	100
South and West								
Aggressive	2	40	1	17	5	20	3	12
Moderate	3	60	5	83				
Nonaggressive					20	80	22	88
Subtotals	5	100	6	100	25	100	25	100
Totals								
Aggressive	33	69	30	60	9	24	7	18
Moderate	15	31	20	40				
Nonaggressive					29	76	31	82
	48	100	50	100	38	100	38	100

Table 5.2
Foreign Policy Scale, Twelfth House, First Session:
Division by Section and Party

	Federalists		Republicans	
	Number	Percent	Number	Percent
Northeast				
Aggressive			12	92
Moderate	3	17		
Nonaggressive	15	83	1	8
Subtotals	18	100	13	100
Middle				
Aggressive	2	15	24	83
Moderate	6	47	5	17
Nonaggressive	5	38		
Subtotals	13	100	29	100
South and West				
Aggressive			39	89
Moderate			2	4
Nonaggressive	6	100	3	7
Subtotals	6	100	44	100
Totals				
Aggressive	2	5	75	87
Moderate	9	24	7	8
Nonaggressive	26	70	4	5
	37	99	86	100

informing him of administrative plans and acting as his agents in government.[9] Throughout 1797 and much of 1798, Adams and his cabinet worked together. By the summer of 1798, however, Hamilton's efforts to become second in command of the army drove a wedge between Adams and a majority of his cabinet. Eventually, Adams demanded the resignations of Pickering, McHenry, and Wolcott, but the period from the summer of 1798 to May of 1800 has long puzzled historians. Concluding that Adams must have known about his cabinet's activities, historians have faulted Adams for indecisiveness and worse.

Many historians account for Adams's reluctance to change his cabinet by citing a determination upon entering office "to make as few removals as possible—not one from personal motives, nor one from party considerations. This resolution I have invariably observed." Stephen Kurtz and Ralph Brown argue that Adams kept the cabinet because of his lack of alternatives; cabinet members were paid extremely low salaries. Gilbert Chinard, however, calls him "naive," and Lawrence Kaplan suggests that had Adams realized what the extent of the disloyalty would become by 1800 he would have cut the cabinet loose in 1797.[10] Peter Shaw's recent biography is the most damning. To Shaw, Adams exhibited "a self-destructive pattern of abrogating power" due to his tendency "to take to his bosom those who delivered [direct aggression]."[11] A comparison with Madison is helpful in resolving this problem.

Madison also began his term without a united cabinet. Preferring to appoint Albert Gallatin as secretary of state, for the sake of party unity he offered the post to Robert Smith. The attempted compromise, however, did not work. Throughout his term, Smith obstructed the administration and finally was cast loose in mid-1811. In contrast to Adams's decision, however, the addition of James Monroe to the cabinet as the new secretary of state restored harmony in the administration and set the stage for the war movement when the Twelfth Congress convened in November.[12]

Madison's strategy succeeded because it stemmed from an overall effort on the part of the president to solidify Republican party cohesion. Indeed, one of the main reasons for the choice of Monroe was to reestablish communication with Congress. Having "honestly" explored the alternatives of commercial restrictions during the Eleventh Congress, Madison and Republicans in the Twelfth Congress turned toward war as the only alternative to national humiliation. In other words, Madison adapted to the changing situation, and the consensus-oriented policies of the war session attest to the effectiveness of his decision.[13]

Madison, in opting to improve member-leader relations in contrast to Adams's pursuit of a more independent course, would seem to have been the more effective leader of the two, especially in terms of group perpetuation and cohesion. Yet Adams also reacted to changing circumstances, and his independence from the cabinet is mirrored in his relations with the Congress. He did not, as Peter Shaw has suggested, lose command of the situation and retreat to

Quincy to "[insulate] himself from the world . . . for escape, not preparation."[14] Following the second session of the Fifth Congress, Adams deliberately isolated himself to protect his independence of action. Therefore, his dismissal of the cabinet was mainly an anticlimactic public admission of what had been a reality in his own mind for some time—he simply was no longer group-oriented.

The crisis in Adams's relationship with the cabinet and the Congress occurred earlier than has previously been noted by historians. The second session of the Fifth Congress brought the high point of the war spirit during the Adams years. In his first message to Congress (and in subsequent speeches after the second session), Adams addressed America's peaceful intentions, the necessity of national unity, the importance of commerce to the nation, and the need for a strong navy.[15] His second speech, on November 23, 1797, concentrated on French intransigence and hostile intentions toward the United States. "There remains no reasonable ground on which to raise an expectation," he warned, "that . . . commerce, without protection or defence, will not be plundered."[16] Then on March 19, 1798, when he submitted the XYZ messages, he reported that he no longer had any hope that the French problems could be settled "on terms compatible with the safety, honor, or the essential interests of the nation." Therefore, he asked Congress "to manifest a zeal, vigor, and concert, in defence of the national rights, proportioned to the degree with which they are threatened."[17] He kept the issue before Congress by submitting additional messages from France (May 4, June 5, and June 18), and in his final message on June 21 he said he presumed that "the negotiation may be considered as at an end."[18]

Still, he never specifically asked for war, and Congress adjourned without declaring open warfare against the French. Adams was looking, it seems, for some degree of unanimity in the Congress. Without a firm legislative stance, he could not in good conscience ask for war. And when the unanimity he hoped for did not materialize, he resorted to peace—a path he faithfully pursued after the summer of 1798.[19] There are many reasons for this lack of unity during the final months of the session. The president could not actively intervene in congressional committees or with influential congressmen as Madison did because committee functions were ill-defined in 1798.[20] Also, the debates of the session reveal a real confusion among Federalists over direction and leadership. On more than one occasion, influential Federalists seemed to work at cross purposes with one another. A group of "Adams Federalists" did not materialize, and he did not listen to the "Hamilton Federalists." Independent of both Republicans and Federalists, he was accused by both groups of partisan attachments he did not possess.

Adams's problems are graphically revealed by comparing the rhetoric of Federalists in 1798 to that of Republicans in 1812. Using the same system of theme analysis that was applied to the prowar speeches of the Twelfth Congress, we examined 2,369 lines of discourse from a sample of five Federalist speakers in the Fifth Congress.[21] The summary of thematic densities for these speeches (Table 5.3), reveals that speakers in 1798 placed greatest emphasis on themes IA1, IC1, IC6, IC8, IIB7, and IIC6. That is, they talked about depredations of commerce, the consequent challenge to the nation's sovereignty, the insincerity of the French, and the possibility of France attacking the United States once it had finished with Great Britain. Notably, the negative effects of French attacks on American commercial interests were singled out for more attention in 1798 than in 1812.

The Federalists' emphasis on commercial interests is revealed even more clearly by the pattern of associations between themes reported in Table 5.4. The most important patterns, involving IA1, IC1, IC6, and IIC7, were combinations of themes related to commercial concerns. Also, attacks on commerce (IA1) were most often discussed directly in terms of national sovereignty (IC8) accompanied by little if any mention of the nation's honor or rights (IC7 and IC5). While Samuel Dana complained that to "abandon our commerce to the depredations of foreigners" reduced the nation "to a state of submission to a foreign Power," Harrison Gray Otis made the point even more bluntly: "If gentlemen should decide that commerce should not be protected, the country would not long be worth the pains of defence; it would become disunited and there would be an end of its propriety." Robert Goodloe Harper added that continued submission would destroy American commerce and the wealth that it brought the nation. In short, Federalists spoke of commerce as first among their priorities and represented national sovereignty merely as the instrument of commercial growth and protection. Without a healthy commerce, they suggested, there was little of value left to justify the continuation of the state. Indeed,

Table 5.3
Thematic Densities (Proportions of Occurrence):
Fifth House, Second Session

Themes	Proportions	Themes	Proportions
IA 1	.080	IIA 1	.023
2	.010	2	.004
3		3	
4	.002	4	.004
5		5	.006
6	.009	Subtotal	.037
7			
Subtotal	.101	B 1	.016
		2	.014
B 1	.013	3	.003
2	.014	4	.002
3		5	
4	.006	6	.004
Subtotal	.033	7	.048
		8	.009
C 1	.117	Subtotal	.096
2	.023		
3		C 1	.002
4	.020	2	.002
5	.018	3	.003
6	.108	4	.001
7	.018	5	.014
8	.125	6	.067
9	.030	7	.018
10	.003	Subtotal	.107
Subtotal	.462		
		Total	.836

Adams's opening address to Congress had reinforced the notion of the preeminence of commerce (a commerce which "made this country what it is") over agriculture, fisheries, arts, and manufactures.[22]

Not surprisingly, the obligation to protect the property of individuals (theme IC6) was linked to threats of secession (theme IC4). As Otis expressed it, "If [asked] to declare whom he [Otis] thought in favor of war, and whose measures led to it, he would say it was those who constantly impeached the Executive authority—who uttered sentiments which had a tendency to dispirit the people, and lead them to believe they could not be defended, and that commerce was

Table 5.4
Association of Themes:
Fifth House, Second Session

IA1 > IA2
     > IC1
     > IC6
     > IC8
     < >IIB7

IIC6 > IC4

IIC7 > IA1
     > IC1
     > IC8

(>)   Indicates that the association
        was established at .10 in only
        one direction, i.e., the theme
        on the left of the sign was
        linked to the theme on the right
        of the sign at least 10% of the
        time but not vice versa.

(< >) Indicates that the association
        was established at .10 in both
        directions.

not worthy of protection." These were measures that led "to war—not to foreign war—but to civil war; a war of friend against friend, and State against State."[23] Even the enemy's hostile motive (theme IIC7), which Federalists associated with attacks on America's commercial interests and national sovereignty (themes IA1, IC1, and IC8), was characterized as a desire to destroy commerce. Overall, Federalists in 1798 did little rhetorically to establish a case for war based on national interests, but chose instead to champion almost exclusively the cause of commercial groups. Narrow material interests, rather than broad concerns over national rights or the survival of the Republic, dominated the rhetoric of Federalist speakers at the high point of the difficulties with France.

A closer look at the language of the Federalists further illustrates how wide the gap was between their characterization of a crisis and the justification for war articulated by Republicans fourteen years later. In contrast to the Republicans, who dramatized the British threat to America via a strategy of diabolism, Federalist rhetors never articulated a threatening image of French attacks (theme IIC6). Their language was laced with relatively unforeboding metaphors of seduction. Unlike Twelfth Congress prowar speakers, who characterized the British by using metaphors of force, Fifth Congress Federalists projected an image of the "seductive" French, a threat which required only that America remain alert and militarily prepared while keeping open the channels of diplomacy.

As members of the Fifth Congress deliberated the question of war, a theme maintained by even the most bellicose speakers was that the French threat would likely yield to a firm American response. Harper, a War Hawk and the foremost orator in Congress, argued that France would "relinquish her aggressions" should the United States follow the "energetic example of the Swiss," whose "spirited conduct" had led to a French withdrawal from their territory. He, along with others, contended that England's recent preparations for the anticipated Gallic invasion had assured against any such attack ever occurring and that similar efforts by the United States would "preserve us from foreign invasion."[24] William Smith argued that "a decided conduct would be the most likely to discourage aggression and repetition of insult." A "firm countenance; not a bullying, but an undaunted attitude" would surely convince the French that "we were not to be threatened out of our rights."[25] The best way to preserve peace, agreed freshman Representative John Dennis, was "to let the Executive go on its own way, in the act of negotiation, while we prepare the means of defending our country."[26] Reaffirming the sentiments of his colleagues, Samuel Sewall, of the House Committee for the Protection of Commerce and the Defence of the Country, added that it was "our weakness, and the division which had appeared in our councils, that had invited these attacks."[27] War could be avoided, in other words, by calling the Directory's bluff.

Federalists spoke regularly of the French threat as primarily one of subversion and seduction, not direct physical confrontation. Acknowledging the power of the French armies, they insisted the Directory lacked the will to attack directly any but the demoralized or disarmed nations of the world. As Harper explained to his constituents in February of 1799, the Directory would not attempt to invade the United States "provided we keep up our preparations and continue to display a firm countenance. Should we be induced, by any deceitful appearance held forth by them, to relax and sink into care-less security, they will think us an easy prey and, no doubt, attempt to devour us." The nation's wisdom, he added a month later, "con-sists in a state of watchful and vigorous preparations."[28] Otis warned of the French nation's nefarious purposes, of its well-known strategy to "divide and command," which had enabled it to "overrun all the republics in the world but our own."[29] Cautioning against French "seduction," William Smith challenged the Congress to resist "the slow approaches to our subjection, by the subtle artifices of intrigue and deception, [which] were seldom discerned by the community at large, until their pestilential effects had taken such deep root as to be with difficulty extirpated."[30]

Two forms of seduction were most worrisome to the Federalists. The first, false appearances of a conciliatory spirit by France, prompted Harper to advocate vigorous military preparations as the best protection against French deceit and artifice. He had told his constituents in July of 1798 that the "only way to avert the danger [of invasion], is to be prepared to meet it; to shew a good countenance, make vigorous preparations, and stand ready to give her a good reception. Seeing this, she may probably keep away." Less than seven months later he was more concerned that "having discov-ered . . . we would not be frightened, she is now trying to coax us." Therefore, he warned, "While we persist in [a] wise policy of keeping the sword unsheathed in one hand and presenting the olive branch with the other, we shall be in no danger. If we depart from it, and suffer ourselves to be lulled into security by any appearances of a conciliatory spirit which France may hold out, we shall share the fate of so many nations, whom she has destroyed more by her deceit-ful artifices than by the force of her arms." Having been already "plundered" by "a nation of robbers," the United States was fore-warned to maintain "a state of watchful and vigorous preparation" while never forgetting that "the Tyger always crouches before he leaps on his prey." The external threat of French seduction could be effectively neutralized by "sounding an alarm" that "opened the eyes" of those who had been "hoodwinked" and "lulled to sleep" by the "opiates" of a deceitful foe. Accordingly, Harper called upon his colleagues "to draw aside the veil" which was "spread before the eyes of the people" and their Congress in an attempt to "blind" them to the necessity of a strong defense.[31]

In its second form, according to the Federalists, French seduction constituted a grievous internal threat. Even if the enemy's infamous diplomatic skills failed to lull the United States into dropping its guard militarily, those same "dark manoeuvres" were also aimed at seducing American citizens into acts of treason.[32] Not only had opposition Republicans performed as French "syrens" by singing their "sweet, enchanting song of policy," but French "intrigues" had also been pushed "into some of the first offices of our Government."[33] Charging that "our bad citizens correspond with the agents of the Directory" who "calculate on individuals here to give efficiency" to French diplomatic means, Otis warned there was no greater danger than from this "system of espionage" and "secret corruption." It was "owing to this cause that all the Republics in Europe had been laid prostrate in the dust; it is this system which has enabled the French to overleap all natural and artificial obstructions; to subjugate Holland and Italy, to destroy the Helvetic Confederacy, and force a passage through rocks and mountains, which have been for ages sacred to the defence of liberty." To avoid the fate of those republics which, subverted by seductive "foreign agents and domestic traitors," had "crumbled into fragments" upon the "slightest shock," Federalists passed the Alien and Sedition Acts in June and July 1798.[34] These repressive measures symbolized well a fear of conspiracy and a desire to "crush the viper in our breast" so that we might "escape the scourge which awaits us."[35]

In sum, France as the object of Federalist metaphors was denounced via diverse but thematically linked vehicles. Comparisons to disease, beasts of prey, and outlaws were effected through terms such as "pestilential," "viper," "Tyger," "devour," "robbers," and "plunder." Peripherally, they conveyed the image of an opportunistic, morally uninhibited foe who could inflict grievous harm upon an unsuspecting victim through either an insidious infection or sudden attack. Most importantly, though, the nucleus of the image consisted of an integrating figure of "seduction," including such terms as "syrens," "wiles," "sweet songs," "veils," "opiates," "hoodwinked," "blinded," "inticed," "duped," "dazzled," "lull," "coax," "snare," "trick," "artifice," "schemes," and "deceit."[36] As it overlapped and focused the implications of more peripheral vehicles, the logic of seduction presupposed a policy of strong defenses and alert diplomacy over direct confrontation as the best preventive against the

"scourge" of foreign domination. So long as the United States resisted the allure of a deadly temptress and left no weak points un-
guarded, there was reason to expect the danger to subside.

In certain respects, Republican metaphors in 1812 were similar
to those which guided Federalist characterizations of the French adversary in 1798. Images of British monsters, murderers, robbers, and
pirates, for instance, paralleled the Federalists' references to French
vipers, robbers, and plunderers. The unifying theme of metaphors in
1812, though, presupposed the enemy's fundamental dependence
upon force rather than deception, a view of the situation that clearly
was more conducive to belligerence. Nothing so refined or civilized
as a French temptress captured the imagination of Republicans in
the war Congress. Instead, with eyes focused on the savagery of
Great Britain, Republicans could envision peace only as a condition
that would lead to their nation's forced enslavement. The image of a
brutal and unrelenting advance toward the center of the nation's
territory made it that much easier to sacrifice the benefits of peace
for the sake of survival. Republicans, unlike their Federalist counterparts in 1798, had drawn upon an archetypal metaphor as their
fundamental source of rhetorical invention. With the image of brute
force, they had turned to one of the bedrocks of symbolism, one of
the "unchanging patterns of experience" to which people are "unusu-
ally susceptible" during "moments of great crisis."[37] Where they succeeded in dramatizing British diabolism (i.e., in giving the enemy's
violent conduct an added sense of presence so that attributions of
evil intentions could be transformed into the "facts" of the situation), Federalist rhetors had adopted as their basic metaphor an image which made the French threat appear to be a bluff that could be
discredited by an alert and prepared nation.

The uses and implications of the metaphor of seduction were as
apparent in the correspondence of Federalists as in their speeches
before Congress. In James Watson's letter to Joel Barlow, express-
ing the sentiments he believed were "generally entertained by the
people" of the United States, the senator from New York informed
the expatriate in Paris that Americans feared France's "invasion less
than her friendship." Having "nearly exhausted its insidious manoeuvres" in order "to perpetuate a state of things by which it gains
much and risks nothing," the Directory now "condescends to spread
new snares for our entanglement." Americans had learned to think

of France "as the beautiful female figure which pierced with darts, and crushed the bones of the victims it embraced."[38] Retired Congressman Stephen Higginson, an influential Massachusetts Federalist and member of the "Essex Junto," reflected both the language and the views of extreme Federalists from the merchant class when he wrote to Timothy Pickering that "Seditions, conspiracies, seductions, and all the Arts which the french use to fraternise and overturn nations, must be guarded against by strong and specific Acts of Congress." In following letters he warned against the "wiles of french diplomacy," the "barefaced trick" and "snare" with which "the Directory have succeeded to intrap the P[resident]," but congratulated the secretary of state for having exposed "french perfidy" in a manner that "stripped off the Veil" and left the French "Villain unmasked."[39]

While Theodore Sedgwick agreed with other High Federalists that "France respected strength alone" and that "the enemy—both foreign and domestic—was quite prepared to take advantage of weakness," he did not agree with them that France would declare war on the United States. If America could avoid being lulled into the trap set by the "chameleon Talleyrand" and would make clear that it had "the power to retaliate," then France would "be conciliatory in earnest." Harper concurred, writing that he was "persuaded that they intend not to make war upon us, but to scourge and frighten us into submission." Even George Cabot, as late as March 26, 1798, wrote to Secretary of the Treasury Wolcott that he was "fully satisfied" France would "never attempt to subdue the United States by force, if she were to see us unitedly determined to resist her with vigor." And by October of the same year, when he indicated to Wolcott his desire for a declaration of war, Cabot still understood that it was "impossible to make the people feel or see distinctly that we have much more to fear from peace than war; that peace cannot be real, and only leaves open a door by which the enemy enters, and that war would shut him out; that the French are wolves in sheep's clothing, entreating to be received as friends, that they may be enabled to destroy and devour." Even though Cabot was now convinced that open and declared war would extinguish the hopes of both "our external enemy" and "internal foes," he had extended the logic of his metaphor beyond the limits accepted by others, including the public in general.[40]

Without the aid of an archetypal metaphor to crystallize the image of national danger and thereby transform particular concerns over commercial depredations into signs of an impending attack on the body politic, the Federalists were easily criticized for championing the interests of the few at the expense of the many. "What," asked William Claiborne of Tennessee, "is the nature of the injuries which we have received? Have they not been wholly maritime?" William B. Giles of Virginia asked further, "Whence . . . arises the clamor for hostile measures—for resistance? Not from our independent yeomanry, nor from men who are the most deeply interested in the welfare of our country, or surrounded with domestic comforts," he answered, "but from men of a different description—from speculators, and men who have few attachments to it." Protection of commerce was not "a sufficient object for which to incur so much risk." In his mind "no nation ought to go to war except when attacked." And, as Nathaniel Smith of Connecticut made clear, he and others did not believe there was any immediate danger of French invasion.[41] Federalists, who without an appeal to diabolism failed to transcend material interests, were thereby unable to establish a publicly acceptable justification for war. Ironically, the failure of Federalists to justify their war measures cast the party into the role of antirepublicans even though they expressly despised the French for abandoning the true principles of republicanism to the excesses of the revolution. The movement toward war stalled, and the establishment of a regular army, the passage of alien and sedition laws, and the enactment of other measures of "defense" reinforced suspicions that these were indeed the expedients of tyranny.[42]

A comparison of the Adams and Madison Congresses, then, indicates many parallels between the two periods and clarifies why war was not declared in 1798. Bloc voting best describes congressional behavior under Adams as under Madison, but this unity did not produce the environment from which Madison's effective leadership evolved. Under Madison, Republicans successfully universalized the threat to the nation with their imperiled-nation logic. Federalists under Adams concentrated their justification almost exclusively on commercial matters and failed to produce a rationale for war that could be defended throughout the nation.

As Alexander DeConde has observed, the public's opposition to war was expressed through both Republicans and moderate Federalists in Congress, making it all but impossible for the president to recommend unlimited hostilities. Adams neither demonstrated the qualities of a "democratic party leader," nor benefited from a unified and tightly organized majority party. Instead, at the close of the second session of the Fifth Congress, Adams believed he would be unable to secure broad support for full-scale war and that it would be "folly for Federalists, with a slender majority in Congress, to rush the country into open war."[43] The Executive and his party simply could not count on public support for a cause that was never adequately couched in the vocabulary of acceptable motives.

After failing in his effort to unify the Congress behind a firmer stance against the French in the spring of 1798, Adams accommodated himself to his independent position and isolated himself from public or party pressures. He was an effective leader because he adapted to changing circumstances; and, had he been president in 1812, he probably would have followed Madison's course.[44] None of the early presidents could have pursued a war under any other justification than that it would unite the nation,[45] and the sense of universality that Federalists failed to establish in 1798 was integral to Madison's decision to pursue war in 1812.

In 1817, Adams, who supported the War of 1812, observed almost wistfully to Jefferson that Madison's presidency "notwithstand[ing] a thousand Faults and Blunders . . . has established more Union, than all his three Predecessors, Washington, Adams and Jefferson, put together."[46] Would, he must have thought, that I could have been president in 1812 rather than in 1798.

CHAPTER SIX

Thomas Jefferson and the Chesapeake Crisis

The Breakdown of Effective Leadership

In 1948 and 1962, Arthur M. Schlesinger conducted a poll of prominent "experts" (55 in 1948 and 75 in 1962, including most of the original 55) in order to determine the "great" American presidents. The respondents, most of whom were historians, rated James Madison as "average" (number 14 in 1948, number 11 in 1962), John Adams as "near great" (number 9 in both polls), and Thomas Jefferson as one of the five "great" presidents (number 5 in both polls.) The Schlesinger tabulations are based on the premise that an ideal, or great, president should possess certain personality traits that make him a great leader. Therefore, strong personalities dominate the upper ranks of the polls, headed by Abraham Lincoln, George Washington, Franklin D. Roosevelt, Woodrow Wilson, and Thomas Jefferson.[1]

This personality orientation is essentially the focus of most books on Jefferson's presidency, including those in recent years by Dumas Malone, Merrill D. Petersen, and Noble E. Cunningham, Jr. Cunningham's most recent book, *The Process of Government under Jefferson*, is a case in point. Based upon extensive reading of the documents of Jefferson's presidency, Cunningham concludes that Jefferson was an effective leader because of the way he coordinated the work of the executive and legislative branches. As the first president "to accept the responsibility of being both the head of the nation and the leader of his party," Jefferson used the Republican party as "a means through which public sentiment could influence public policy." The key element in this effort was the cabinet, the members of which were expected to be presidential advisors and liaisons with the Congress, especially the congressional committees. Effectively, the cabinet was "the central mechanism of executive administration." But, in turn, the cabinet functioned successfully only due to Jefferson's talent for system and organization, discussion and persuasion. As president, he had the ability to keep men working together.[2]

Because of these successful leadership traits (all a function of his personality), Jefferson's administration, for Cunningham, stands as an integrated system spanning the entire eight years of his presidency. To be sure, changes occurred, as when the president could not find anyone to take John Randolph's place as informal floor leader in the House after 1806 and when the embargo brought divisiveness into the Republican ranks, but overall "the structure of government changed very little during [Jefferson's] eight years in office." And his management of the government was better than that of either of the men who preceded and followed him. Adams did not know how to use the cabinet effectively, and Madison could not continue Jefferson's "strong presidential leadership, Cabinet effectiveness, party viability, and successful working relationships between the executive and Congress."[3]

The problem with assessing leadership ability primarily on the basis of personality characteristics is that the environmental factors which also shape the president's actions receive little attention. As has been noted in chapter 2, recent behavioral studies of leadership conclude that a person's actions as a leader are determined more by the situation than by personality factors. Such a view is especially valuable for Jefferson's presidency because of the discontinuities of his two administrations. The events of the second administration were largely divorced from those of the first term. Domestic matters—especially the struggle with the judiciary and the implementation of Republican ideology in the nation's economic affairs— dominated the first four years whereas foreign policy affairs consumed most of Jefferson's attention after 1805. Simultaneously with this extreme shift in emphasis, Jefferson's leadership behavior also changed. Early in his administration he was extremely group-oriented, meeting frequently with his cabinet and members of Congress. The closer the day of his retirement came, however, the more aloof and detached he became from public affairs. Ideas, which directed his behavior throughout his life, became less and less the determinants of policy as events moved more and more out of control, falling hard upon one another beginning the summer of 1807 and defying simplistic explanations.

In short, there were two Jeffersons occupying the presidency, one adroitly directing the affairs of state by creatively influencing the actions of others, the other controlled by and reacting to situations. In contrast to John Adams, who also became increasingly less group-oriented during the war crisis with France in 1798, Jefferson expected partisanship to carry the nation through the English crisis of 1807 without realizing that the group loyalty of 1800 had been severely eroded by the time of the attack on the *Chesapeake*. Preoccupation with the Burr trial, a false assumption that the Congress would do what the administration advised, and an unwillingness to involve himself personally in legislative-executive relationships combined to negate Jefferson's ability to lead the nation to a solution of its foreign policy problems. And the Republicans in Congress, forced back upon themselves for solutions, found that they could not agree upon a sufficiently threatening image of British hostility to warrant a call to arms. As with the Adams Congresses, therefore, leadership, partisanship, and rhetoric did not combine to produce a declaration of war.

Three recent views of Jefferson's presidency well describe the discontinuity between his two administrations. Robert M. Johnstone, Jr. uses Richard Neustadt's theory of role analysis to assess Jefferson's leadership effectiveness as president. In role analysis, success as a leader is measured more by the influence the president had on others than by the actions themselves. In Jefferson's use of the political party during his first term, Johnstone argues that Jefferson united the branches of government and "enlarged the horizons of acceptable political behavior." As president, Jefferson was less the philosopher directed by a "narrowly doctrinaire [view] . . . of the proper limits of power" than a man of public affairs "acutely attuned to the art of the possible." Thus, his leadership of the Republican party coincided nicely with the problems of running the capital community. Entertaining congressmen, using the cabinet—especially Secretary of the Treasury Albert Gallatin—to guide Congress, appointing floor leaders in the House, and the use of his personal reputation allowed Jefferson to rule effectively as president.[4]

Therefore, Johnstone argues, when Jefferson announced that he would not run again as president beyond the second term, he undermined his success as president by destroying his leadership of the party. Leadership of the Republican party had been the "central factor in the party's remarkable unity," and with the embargo, the strains on the leader-led relationship became paralyzing. Jefferson tried to control all of the factors of the situation by personal will rather than by a "situational and interactional" direction of the nation's affairs. Finally, during the second session of the Tenth Congress, Jefferson withdrew completely from the direction of public affairs, claiming that he did so to leave Madison a free hand in directing policy. A desire to escape conflict or sheer pride may have paralyzed the president. Whatever the reason, his behavior "conflicts sharply with the keen sensitivity to power resources that he expressed and displayed on most other occasions during his presidency."[5]

Similar conclusions emerge from Burton Spivak's and Drew R. McCoy's recent reassessments of Jefferson's foreign policy. Spivak argues that interpretations of Jefferson's presidency are changing as historians focus less on his interest in and contributions to political freedom than on his interest in the social order "and the transition from 'virtuous citizen' to 'commercial man.' "[6] As a reflective colonial, Jefferson was interested both in liberty and what McCoy calls "political economy." Unfortunately, these two intellectual interests were not totally compatible. "Balanced against his liberal faith in man's moral capacity for self-government was a conservative emphasis on the fragility of this capacity and on the proper social order necessary for its development." What became the "central theme" of Jefferson's life, according to Spivak, was "an attempt to make commerce compatible with republicanism," a possibility only when commerce was as closely connected with agriculture as possible. Farmers and merchants had to be bound into an "equal and tranquil partnership."[7]

During Jefferson's presidency, however, protecting the carrying trade—the transport of French and Spanish goods between colonies and mother countries—became increasingly important. John Randolph argued that the carrying trade was "totally unconnected with agriculture, and enjoyed by a few merchants only," but Jefferson defended the trade primarily for political and emotional reasons.

"Not to defend it," Spivak argued, "involved significant political risks and to defend it successfully seemed only to require a strong legal and moral argument on its behalf." Therefore, Jefferson was willing to leave the Congress to formulate policy after 1805 and approved of the embargo initially in order to buy time for the development of a new policy, not to use economic coercion to secure American rights. The policies of 1808 show, to Spivak, the bankruptcy of Jefferson's political solution to the problem of defending the carrying trade. The embargo and its enforcement indicate "a false bravado, almost like children whistling past the graveyard. . . . Merely to threaten war, it appears, was the extent of their belligerence." In the end, Jefferson failed to resolve the nation's problems because of psychological inadequacies. He was blinded by "an abstract rationality" created by the "seductive logic of [his] own policies." He was "trapped in the logic and decency of [his] own fictions . . . of morality and justice," and did not consider the legitimacy of England's position.[8]

McCoy is less harsh, arguing that the embargo signified the conversion of Jefferson and his party to a mercantilistic rather than a free trade solution to the nation's economic problems. "The Jeffersonian endeavor to secure a peaceful, predominantly agricultural republic demanded a tenaciously expansive foreign policy—a foreign policy that ultimately endangered both the peace and the agricultural character of the young republic." And with war in 1812, Jeffersonians (but not Jefferson, completely) discarded a market salvation for the American republic based on agricultural production for Alexander Hamilton's view of domestic markets and manufacturing. What began, therefore, as a "necessary means of furthering the Revolutionary vision of free trade" ended in the creation of a manufacturing solution to "vindicate the promise of a republican political economy." Republicans fought, and won, the wrong war.[9]

With regard to the question of Jefferson's effectiveness as president, each of these assessments concludes that a substantial difference exists between the president's behavior in the two terms caused by Jefferson's failure to continue to utilize the resources of leadership employed early in his administration. Had Jefferson acted during the embargo debate as he did earlier in his presidency, he might have succeeded in arriving at a suitable reconciliation of the nation's problems. Instead, personal factors led Jefferson to fail to direct the foreign policy events of his second term. Cunningham believes Jefferson did not act because he so resented Adams's actions during the last months of his presidency. Jefferson's behavior to Johnstone is an "enigma" that may be explained best by the psychological explanation of pride and the inability to accept conflict. For Spivak, rationalization and personal and political frustrations hold the key to understanding Jefferson's actions after 1805. McCoy shows how Jefferson and his party were unable to control events and in the end were controlled by them. In short, Jefferson failed because he refused to adapt his leadership to changing circumstances.

Thus, Cunningham, Johnstone, Spivak, and McCoy all settle on personality or ideological reasons for Jefferson's change in behavior after 1806. It is possible that Jefferson's personality overcame his earlier style of leadership based on group consensus, but there is an alternative explanation for why he failed to adapt his leadership as president to changing situations. Early in his career, the situation of the country and the party was conducive to a leadership strategy that solidified the unity of the party and translated it into what social psychologists Fred E. Fiedler and Martin Chemers call "task-oriented" policies.[10] After 1805, however, when the party was factionalized by the Yazoo land controversy, the inevitable divisions over Jefferson's successor in 1808, and the detrimental and eventually destructive change in international relations between England and France, Jefferson discarded his "relationship-orientation" for an extreme, task-oriented leadership style. When the nation's (and the party's) interests once again demanded good leader-follower relations, Jefferson was preoccupied with events and thereby allowed the situation to control his behavior. When the *Chesapeake* affair demanded his attention, his good relations with the Congress had long since evaporated, and his attention was already focused on a different problem. Jefferson could not deal flexibly with the foreign policy crisis in June of 1807 because he was already preoccupied to the point of distraction with the trial of Aaron Burr.

One of the strangest facts about the literature on Jefferson's presidency is that historians refuse to link two events that occurred almost simultaneously—the Burr trial and the attack on the *Chesapeake*. Ironically, Dumas Malone begins his chapter on the evolution of the embargo with the statement that "the synchronization of historical events in the summer of 1807 is a fascinating exercise and a very necessary one if their interrelation is to be understood," but he is referring only to the meeting two weeks after the *Chesapeake* incident between Napoleon and Alexander I.[11] The Burr episode is dealt with two hundred pages earlier. Similarly, Burton Spivak divorces his moment-by-moment analysis of Jefferson's attempts at leadership of foreign policy in the summer of 1807 from the Burr materials.[12] Jefferson never indicated specifically that the *Leopard*'s attack on the *Chesapeake* was timed to coincide with the Burr trial, but he did view them as a happy coincidence. His external enemies, the British, and his internal enemies, the Federalists, could finally be dealt with together.

During the height of preparations for Burr's trial (and immediately following a week of headaches that incapacitated him), Jefferson wrote to Tench Coxe that he did not expect "any serious attempts" against the republican form of government from European nations. "They have," he wrote, "too many jealousies of one another, to engage in distant wars for a matter of opinion only."[13] One month later, however, his mind was changing as a result of supposed Federalist intrigues to destroy republicanism through the Federalist-controlled judiciary. Good would come, he wrote, even if Burr were pardoned in Richmond because the trial would then be a way of convincing the people that the courts should not be above public control. The Burr trial, in other words, would become the agent for a complete exorcism of Federalism from the republican experiment in government.[14]

Great Britain must have either sensed that the Federalists were losing their last bastion of power or simply blundered into a situation that could be used to highlight the British threat to the nation's existence. Either way, the events of June would serve a useful purpose. If the magnitude of Burr's capture and trial may be said to have given Jefferson his headaches, the *Chesapeake* incident certainly cleared his mind and charted his course. At last, the enemies of the nation would be known. War would unite the nation as the shots fired at Lexington had in 1775.[15] What is most striking about Jefferson's correspondence beginning in June of 1807 is not the content but the tone. Everything was crystal clear. All ambiguities were wiped away by the "extraordinary occurrence and the state of things that brings on."[16]

The one thing Jefferson did not anticipate, however, was the

Congress's response. Based upon research two decades ago by Bradford Perkins and most recently by Burton Spivak, one must conclude that Jefferson wanted war in the summer of 1807.[17] Unfortunately for Jefferson, the first session of the Tenth Congress, which followed the attack on the *Chesapeake*, was not a propitious period for a declaration of war. In a letter to Madison on August 20, 1807, Jefferson spoke of how he intended to approach the Tenth Congress. Rejecting Albert Gallatin's more moderate proposal that the *Chesapeake* matter not be put before Congress prior to hearing something from England, Jefferson believed that "on the meeting of Congress, we should lay before them everything that has passed to that day, and place them on the same ground of information we are on ourselves. *They will then have time to bring their minds to the same state of things with ours, and when the answer arrives, we shall all view it from the same position* [emphasis added]." In other words, Congress would naturally support the administration's position as it had in the first term.[18]

But the unanimity of purpose Jefferson expected did not materialize. The second session of the Ninth Congress had witnessed the nadir of Republican unity in the House, and the wounds had not healed. Cross-bloc voting, which had not occurred prior to the session, was more apparent in the votes of representatives from the middle states during that session than elsewhere, but confusion abounded in all sections except the South and West. Furthermore, a scale of votes prior to the adoption of the embargo indicates that a wide diversity of opinion existed regarding the best strategy to be pursued.[19] Local politics, especially the factionalism that swirled around Albert Gallatin in Pennsylvania, the Clinton family in New York, and the Smith family in Maryland, may have been responsible for much of this congressional confusion, but the point is that the Republicans in the Congress would have to be unified before they would follow any directive of the president, much less a movement toward war.

Simply put, Jefferson did not try to rebuild party unity because he felt he did not have to. Surely all would see the threat posed by the Federalists in the Burr trial and the English in the attack on the *Chesapeake* in the same way he did. On October 8 he wrote to Robert Smith, "Everything we see and hear leads in my opinion to war; we have therefore much to consult and determine on preparatory to that event."[20] But the meeting of Congress dashed his hopes. Gallatin convinced the president to tone down his annual message, and the House opted for the peaceful tone of the message rather than the belligerent cast of the president's intent. On November 1 the president reported to William H. Cabell, "Here we are pacifically inclined, if anything comes which will permit us to follow our inclinations." Congress was left to itself, and by December Jefferson had reconciled himself to the "snail-paced gait for the advance of new ideas on the general mind." He wrote that Congress was in no hurry to act: "If too hard pushed, they balk, and the machine retrogrades." At best the embargo was a device to clear the seas of American ships and to buy time for war preparations, and it was probably more Madison's or Gallatin's idea than Jefferson's. Neither the leadership tactics nor the extreme party unity of the first term was present in 1807, and Jefferson retreated from war.[21]

As with the Adams Congresses, when the majority party Republicans were left to themselves to make sense out of the nation's affairs, they found that they lacked a language with which to define the immediate threat to the nation posed by Great Britain. That is, in addition to fissures within the party and a lack of relationship-oriented leadership from the executive, the posture taken by Republican rhetors also prevented further progress toward a declaration of war. Republicans did manage to appeal to the broad interests of the public as they attempted to gather support for an increasingly belligerent attitude toward foreign encroachments. Still, though, no clear image of diabolism emerged from their discourse to justify the final break with Great Britain. Unlike the Federalists of '98, Republicans opened the Tenth Congress with a call to defend their country's rights and honor—for the sake of the republic, not just its commerce. Like their Federalist predecessors, however, these champions of nation-wide interests portrayed the adversary's intentions as subject to influence by means short of war. Without the threat of immediate danger, war remained only a possibility rather than a necessity. An important step toward justifying war had been taken, yet the language was still that of the pre-, not the prowar rhetor. To better understand the inherent constraints as well as the potentialities of this language, we turn now to a more detailed account of the themes and images with which Republicans defined their options following the attack on the *Chesapeake*.

Our analysis of 3,593 lines of discourse, representing five speeches sampled from the first session of the Tenth Congress, confirms that Republicans stressed some of the same themes as had Federalists ten years earlier—including themes related to depredations on commerce, mistreatment of seamen, and plans to attack the United States.[22] The Republicans, though, also gave new or added attention to themes IA2, IA3, IC5, IC7, IC9, IIA4, and IIB8 (Table 6.1).[23] In other words, commerce received less than the almost exclusive attention it had attracted in 1798. Britain's attack on the *Chesapeake* (IA3) was added to the list of complaints; considerably more

Table 6.1
Thematic Densities (Proportions of Occurrence):
Tenth House, First Session

Themes	Proportions	Themes	Proportions
IA 1	.096	IIA 1	.008
2	.081	2	
3	.031	3	
4	.003	4	.036
5	.005	5	___
6	.007	Subtotal	.044
7	___		
Subtotal	.223	B 1	.005
		2	.001
B 1		3	
2	.006	4	
3		5	
4	.001	6	
Subtotal	.007	7	.013
		8	.025
C 1	.028	Subtotal	.044
2			
3		C 1	.001
4		2	
5	.027	3	
6	.005	4	.020
7	.033	5	.019
8	.036	6	.072
9	.060	7	___
10	.008	Subtotal	.111
Subtotal	.197		
		Total	.626

attention was given to the impressment of sailors (IA2); and damage to commerce (IC1 and IC6) received much less notice than in the Fifth Congress. Moreover, added emphasis was placed on national rights and honor (IC5 and IC7), and Republicans made a greater attempt to vindicate America of any wrongdoing than had Federalists (IIA4). There was also a relatively frequent but generalized suggestion of a possible attack by Great Britain (IIC6).

Also, as Table 6.2 indicates, majority party speakers in 1807–08 (unlike Federalists in 1798) did not link their discussion of attacks against commerce (IA1) directly to questions of sovereignty (IC8). Instead, concern over national honor (IC7) and sovereignty was associated with the issue of national rights (IC5), which itself was discussed in terms of depredations on commerce (IA1). National honor and independence, that is, were considered at risk because of the challenge to America's rights represented by the depredation of American commerce—a matter of far more universal significance than the interests of commercial groups could ever become in isolation. Richard M. Johnson underscored this relation between the nation's sov-

Table 6.2
Association of Themes:
Tenth House, First Session

IA1	>	IC1
IA2<	>	IA3
IC5	>	IA1
	>	IA2
	< >	IC7
	< >	IC8
	>	IC9
IC7<	>	IC8
	< >	IC9
IC8	>	IIA4
IC9	>	IIC4
	< >	IIC6

(>) Indicates that the association was established at .10 in only one direction, i.e., the theme on the left of the sign was linked to the theme on the right of the sign at least 10% of the time but not vice versa.

(<>) Indicates that the association was established at .10 in both directions.

ereignty, honor, and rights when he proclaimed that "should this nation be compelled to take up arms, the people were unanimous; they were pledged by their resolution to support measures of the Government consistent with the nation's honor and the nation's rights"; bound by their "sacred principles of patriotism," the people "would defend their independence at the hazard of life and property."[24] John Love explained further that America's rights were at stake because the French Decrees and British Orders (theme IA1) constituted "an unjustifiable attack," a "peculiar mode of warfare which has proved so destructive to the rights of neutrals" (theme IC5).[25] Even the motives that were imputed to the adversary (IIC4 and IIC6) and associated with references to America's troubles (IC9) highlighted both British hostility and plans to attack the nation as a whole rather than just the desire to destroy a rival commerce.

In short, there emerged a clear tendency in the Tenth Congress toward universalizing the foreign threat by linking Britain's hostile actions against commerce to the broader issue of America's national rights and then assessing the denial of rights as a challenge to American sovereignty. Whereas Federalists had tried to justify hostilities with France on narrow grounds, appealing almost singularly to the economic motive of protecting commerce, Republicans considered commercial interests but subsumed them within a more general call to protect the nation's honor, safety, and rights. Despite this movement toward the prowar stance, however, Republican efforts fell short of justifying war when no corresponding strategy of diabolism was developed to establish the existence of a breach that defied repair.

Without the aid of an appeal to diabolism, an otherwise belligerent George W. Campbell was forced into the position of saying, "I do not wish to be understood . . . as having any desire to go to war—no, I do not—but I trust the people of America are determined never to surrender or barter their honor, their rights, or independence for a shameful peace."[26] In other words, he perceived a potential threat to national sovereignty in the attacks on American commerce and other wrongs suffered at the hands of the British, but it was not yet severe or compelling enough to justify a final appeal for war. The choice, though, already had been narrowed to one of war or embargo, and more restrained responses to British harassments represented nothing short of submission. Philip B. Key presented the Federalist view that the United States should "pursue the steady line of rigid impartiality" between France and England by trading "with all who will trade with us. Much of the world is yet open to us," he suggested, "and let us profit of the occasion."[27] Outraged, David R. Williams cried out on behalf of the House Republicans, "What sir! Succumb to Great Britain, kiss the hem of her garment, and let her direct your trade where she pleases, under penalty of being liable to seizure if her vessels come across it! Heaven forbid it! . . . The nation will have no character—it will be degraded if we submit to this."[28] Johnson added that America could no longer hold on to the claim of independence if it would not now maintain its rights.[29] Just as in 1812, the issue was reduced to a question of "assertion of rights or submission to aggression."[30] Without a supporting image of British diabolism, though, embargo could not be dismissed as a viable means of asserting the nation's rights, and when Congress adjourned in April 1808, the prevailing image of Britain still allowed for the possibility of favorably influencing its unfriendly disposition toward America by means of economic coercion.

A foundation for the strategy of diabolism, however, was laid in this first session of the Tenth Congress as members debated the merits of economic coercion. While Republicans agreed, for the most part, that there was adequate cause for war, they remained unsettled over how to resolve the issue of culpability. It was argued that by not taking firm economic measures of resistance to British encroachments the United States had encouraged continued transgressions against its commercial rights. As James Fisk complained, "I believe most religiously, that had it not been for sentiments expressed in this country so favorable to Great Britain; had it not been for insinuations that it was impossible for us to maintain this measure [of embargo], before this time we would have been treated with respect by Great Britain."[31] A firmer stand, that is, would cause England to recede.

The argument that hostile British policies and intentions were subject to the influence of firm economic sanctions echoed throughout the House chamber. According to Campbell, the embargo was designed to bring the English "to a just estimate of their own interests, and a sense of justice toward us." Economic measures were an overdue step toward declaring the nation's determination to resist aggression.[32] Representative John Rhea agreed, calling the embargo a "system of peace" imposed to show that the United States was determined to preserve and support its neutrality.[33] "Adhere, sir, to this measure with firmness," contended Thomas Newton, who headed the House Committee of Commerce and Manufactures, "and the accommodation of our differences will be certain and advantageous."[34] Thus, firm adherence to the embargo was presented as a way to convince Great Britain that the United States would not yield its claim to neutral rights and that those rights therefore should be respected. The embargo promised to free the United States from any blame for the crisis while placing the burden on England to prove its intentions. A basis for testing British intentions had been devised.

The significance of the embargo as a test of British intentions and a key to developing the image of diabolism emerges clearly out of the correspondence of Burwell Bassett, Republican Congressman from Virginia, to Joseph Prentis. On February 25, 1808, he wrote that the British

> must be made to feel the pressure of a restrained commerce before they will open their eyes to what justice to us and their own good requires. Such is the demonial influence of jealousy that it even injures itself and the object it most wishes to cherish. Thus merchants are ardent to monopolise. To this use the British whould subvert the seas and are blind to the fatal blow they are giving to commerce itself and regardless of the terrible reacction it will have on themselves. To Britain commerce is every thing it is interwoven with the national debt and the resources of the country are so dependant on it that as with commerce they have risen so with it they must decline. Bonaparte has certainly without intending favor to our republic given us a strong hold on Britain. Having lost the continental trade that of America has become of the best importance to Britain. It is no longer a convenience it has become necessary to the existance of the many hands hitherto employed in the commerce of the continent and America equal to nearly five sixths of the whole British trade It cannot be doubted that a judicious use of this power will bring England to her senses & convince her of the futility of attempting to appropriate . . . the common highway to her own use.[35]

If Britain did not come to its senses after feeling the effects of the embargo, Bassett's letter implied, there was good reason to conclude that the demon of commercial jealousy and the desire to monopolize had overwhelmed that nation's rational faculties and placed it beyond the influence of pacific measures.

Certainly, the language of Republican orators allowed for the inference that Britain would eventually force its will on the nation rather than succumb to attempts at economic coercion. The image of a beast of prey combined with attributions of criminality were featured in George Washington Campbell's depiction of Britain's earlier attack on Denmark. Campbell warned that the "so much famed British lion, stretched forth his merciless paw, fastened its fangs upon her capital, murdered her people, and robbed her of her Navy."[36] Joseph Desha suggested, somewhat tentatively, "it appears that we must either passively submit to have our inherent rights wrested from our hands, by those haughty free-booters, or resort to that dreadful alternative, war."[37] Drawing upon similar images of force, Johnson complained to his constituents that American seamen were being "torn from their families, their friends, their country," and that "all the kindred ties of the human heart [were being] broken asunder by a British press gang."[38] James Fisk of Vermont used the metaphor of force to interpret Great Britain as saying, "I have abused you; humble yourself, succumb to me, and I will make such satisfaction as I think fit."[39] In every sea, Desha warned, "the gigantic strength of her navy has enabled her to trample the rights of neutrals under her feet."[40] Even so, proclaimed John Eppes, his country would refuse "to bend to lawless power."[41]

It took Republicans another three years before they began to realize the full potential of their language and new logic for establishing the fixed and hostile motives of Great Britain. In the meantime, the nation had to prove its "determination to resist aggressions," in the words of Campbell, before it could be sure that England was a determined foe. It appeared to Campbell that "a tissue of aggravated insults" existed. "Had not one aggression been committed after another in regular succession, and with increasing atrocity, until the climax of aggravated injury was completed by the attack on the Chesapeake?" To him, "it would seem as if the object of that nation was to mock negotiation." Still, though he would not rely on it alone, Campbell continued to express considerable confidence in the embargo.[42] Newton agreed, despite his suspicion that "monopoly of commerce" was the object that the "iniquitous orders of her Cabinet have been issued to obtain."[43] First, though, as John Rhea emphasized, "Let us show that we are determined to preserve and support our neutrality."[44] The implication, of course, was that Britain's diabolism would be proved by its perseverence in attacking

American commerce despite whatever damage was caused by the embargo to the British economy. The test could be only as good as a firm adherence to the embargo would allow, and Americans soon discovered the difficulty of upholding their part of the examination. In 1807–08 only the potential for drawing on the nation's vocabularies of acceptable motives had been established by Republicans who addressed the question of war.

Thus the Jefferson Congress which dealt with the *Chesapeake* affair stands somewhere between the Adams Congresses and the war session under Madison. In terms of leadership and partisanship, more similarities exist with the Adams years. Neither Adams nor Jefferson acted directly to improve leader-group relations in the war crisis situations, and party unity was shallow, at best, in both periods. Rhetorically, however, the themes and persuasive techniques of Republican speakers were much closer to those used in the war session than to those used in the Fifth Congress.

No substantial change occurred with regard to any of these factors—leadership, partisanship, and rhetoric—during the last two years of Jefferson's presidency, but it is interesting to note that Jefferson did devote much of his time after leaving the presidency to rebuilding the party unity he failed to rekindle while president. In letters to *Aurora* editor William Duane and others who threatened to split the party on foreign policy matters, Jefferson preached party unity as the salvation of the nation. "Some think," he wrote to Duane early in 1811, "that independence (of action) requires them to follow always their own opinion, without respect to others. This has never been my opinion, nor my practice." If Republicans would not "act in phalanx, as when we rescued [the nation] from the satellites of monarchism, I will not say our *party*, the term is false and degrading, but our *nation* will be undone. For the republicans are the *nation*. . . . You know, my dear sir, that this union of republicans has been the constant theme of my exhortations."[45] Thus, when the war came, Jefferson enthusiastically endorsed it as providing "indemnity for the past, security for the future, and compleat emancipation from Anglomany, Gallomany, and all the manias of demoralized Europe."[46]

In none of these letters, however, did Jefferson acknowledge that most of the standard causes of the war with Great Britain—impressment, defense of neutral rights, and protection of the nation's honor—were more directly affronted by the British in the attack on the *Chesapeake* than during the war session of the Twelfth Congress. If Jefferson accepted war in 1812, as he did, he should have pursued it more actively in 1807, or even in 1809 when the embargo was repealed. Instead, when members of the congressional majority failed to see the world as he did—a view greatly intensified by the Burr trial—the president retreated into himself and refused to exercise the effective leadership skills that he had mastered during his first term. If Jefferson had been more of a rhetorical leader as well as more of a relationship-oriented president, war might have been declared following the attack on the *Chesapeake*. But in the absence of this leadership, it took Republicans four more years to develop the unity of purpose and the words with which to express the immediacy of the British threat to the nation. The ensuing chapters discuss these two issues.

CHAPTER SEVEN

Establishing a Behavioral Link between the Embargo and War

The embargo of 1807 divided the nation at the time, and controversy surrounding its authorship, its implementation, and its successes and failures still exists.[1] Concerning one aspect of the embargo's history, however, there is consensus—somehow, the repeal of the embargo led to war in 1812. Burton Spivak, in his recent reappraisal of Jefferson's policies of economic coercion, concludes that the repeal of the embargo per se did not lead to war, but rather that the humiliation the nation suffered under nonintercourse gave "another reason apart from foreign oppression and the girth of its dream for 'prosperous neutrality' to go, finally, to war." Bradford Perkins is more direct: the failure of the embargo merely delayed "the outbreak of war with England—and that, until a less favorable time." Somewhere between these two is Roger Brown, who argues that neither the failure of the embargo nor nonintercourse, singly or in combination, led directly to war. Rather, war was the logical result of the failure of commercial restriction to compel respect for neutral rights.[2]

The purpose of this chapter is to test the validity of these arguments by comparing the voting behavior of majority party Republicans in the second session of the Tenth Congress with their counterparts in the first session of the Twelfth Congress. If it is true that the embargo's repeal is related to the war movement, it should be possible to establish a behavioral link between the two periods.

A graph of Republican cohesion across the second session of the Tenth Congress indicates that voting may be divided into three phases. During the first two months of the session, Republicans recorded a higher level of cohesion than at any other time, falling below an index of 50 (72/25 percent split) on only two of the thirty-

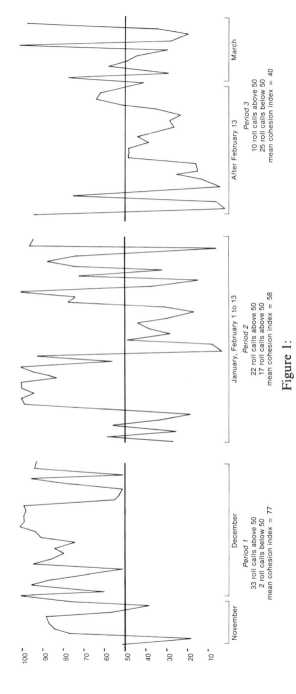

Figure 1:

Republican Party Indexes of Cohesion: Tenth House, Second Session

five roll calls (6 percent) and attaining an average index of 77 for the period (88.5/11.5 percent split; see Figure 1).[3] Beginning in early January, however, party unity dropped, was reachieved, and then fluctuated wildly through late January and early February. During this period, Republicans fell below an index of 50 seventeen of thirty-nine times (44 percent) and averaged an index of 58 (79/21 percent split). Then, from mid-February through the end of the session, overall Republican cohesion slipped to approximately half of its original levels (40, or a 70/30 percent split), and the party fell below the 50 mark on twenty-five of thirty-five roll calls (71 percent).

Shifts in Republican voting behavior can further be demonstrated by constructing cluster-blocs for each of the three periods. Table 7.1 shows the change in bloc sizes over the three periods examined.

Table 7.1
Bloc Sizes Across the Session:
Tenth House, Second Session

	Period	Federalists			Republicans		
		Bloc	+ Fringe	= Total	Bloc	+ Fringe	= Total
1.	Nov. – Dec.	30	4	34	78	8	86
2.	Jan. – Feb. 13	32	7	39	72	14	86
3.	After Feb. 13	52	7	59	29	32	61

As noted with regard to the cohesion indexes, the decline in Republican cohesion from period one to period two is not nearly so dramatic as it is in the period following February 13.

To be sure, the Federalist bloc (including fringe) gained five legislators, but Republican cohesion remained virtually constant in the first two periods. After February 13, however, Federalist bloc size increased dramatically. The corresponding decline in Republican bloc size and overall cohesion meant that by the end of the session the two blocs were virtually equal whereas Republicans had originally outnumbered their antagonists more than two to one.

That a shift of Republicans to the Federalist position was responsible for the embargo's repeal seemed clear to at least one interested observer in February of 1809. On February 7 and 8, 1809, President Thomas Jefferson reported "a sudden and unaccountable revolution of opinion . . . chiefly among the New England & New York members." Not only had they voted "in a kind of panick" to support

March 4 as the date for the repeal of the embargo, but their majority "gave all reason to believe they would not agree either to war or nonintercourse." Worst of all for Jefferson was the *timing* of the "revolution." The president lamented that the change in voting had occurred "after we had become satisfied that the Essex Junto had found their expectation desperate, of inducing the people . . . to either separation or forcible opposition." Great Britain "through her omnipotence over our Commercial men" had managed "to shake our Union, to it's center, to controul it's legislative & Executive authorities, . . . and perhaps to constrain us to unconditional submission to her will."[4]

The harshness of Jefferson's tone and his interest in explaining this "unaccountable revolution" did not pass quickly. In July of 1810, Jefferson reconstructed the final days of the session and again castigated the Federalists for their seditious appeals to New Englanders to resist the embargo. But he lay the blame for the embargo's repeal at the feet of New England Republicans, led by

> one pseudo-Republican, [Joseph] Story. He came on (in the place of [Jacob] Crowninshield, I believe) and staid only a few days, long enough however to get complete hold of [Ezekiel] Bacon, who giving in to his representations, became panick struck, & communicated his panick to his colleagues [from New England] & they to a majority of the sound members of Congress.[5]

Burton Spivak's recent account of the embargo's repeal also emphasizes the influence of Federalist anti-embargo tactics on Story's actions. Spivak argues, however, that Story's, Bacon's, and the other New Englanders' thinking was determined by John Quincy Adams, whose correspondence with the men from Massachusetts helped cause, and also charted, New England's retreat from the embargo. Combined with Story's arrival in December, Adams's fears of the "internal turmoil" caused by the embargo and Federalist use of the issue in Massachusetts politics "framed the retreat from the embargo in a socially valid context, and anchored [Massachusetts Republicans'] longings to escape the embargo to a respected New England authority figure."[6]

One way to uncover what happened in early February is to compare the voting blocs of the three periods to see which congressmen shifted from Republican to Federalist positions (Table 7.2). Four-

Table 7.2
Legislators Who Changed Blocs:
Tenth House, Second Session

Legislators	State	Blocs by Period		
		1	2	3
Two Changes				
Cook	Ma	R	X	F
Hoge	Pa	F	R	F
Smith, S.	Pa	X	R	F
Helms	NJ	R	X	F
Mumford	Ma	R	X	F
Swart	Ma	R	X	F
Thompson	Ma	R	X	F
Stanford	NC	X	F	R
One Change				
Bacon	Ma		R	F
Barker	Ma		R	F
Ilsley	Ma		R	F
Wilbour	RI		R	F
Durell	NH		R	F
Storer	NH		R	F
Hiester	Pa		R	F
McCreery	Md		R	F
Van Horne	Md		R	F
Boyd	NJ		R	F
Sloan	NJ		R	F
Southard	NJ		R	F
Blake	NY		R	F
Humphrey	NY		R	F
Riker	NY		R	F
Van Alen	NY		R	F
Van Cortlandt	NY		R	F
Verplanck	NY		R	F
Wilson	NY		R	F
Bassett	Va		F	R
Macon	NC		F	R

F = Federalist   X = Cross-bloc
R = Republican   Fringe counts as bloc

teen of the twenty-six who changed from Republican to Federalist blocs (54 percent) were from New England or New York, and Orchard Cook *was* the first New Englander (as Spivak indicates) to change to the Federalist bloc. What Jefferson's statements and Spivak's analysis overlook, however, is the possibility that some other issue than fears of the Federalists in the North was responsible for the repeal of the embargo. The graph of Republican voting in the session (Figure 1) indicates that the decline in Republican cohesion that occurred after February 13 was foreshadowed by an extreme downturn in late December and early January. It is only when one investigates the issue that first confused the party—the question of whether to increase the role of the navy in the nation's foreign policy—that the reasons for repealing the embargo and the importance of the repeal to the movement to war in 1812 become clear.

Jefferson was quite correct in fingering Bacon and Story for leading the change in voting, but he mistook the timing of these two men's "revolution." During debates on a bill to prohibit foreign licenses for U.S. ships on December 29, 1808, both Story and Bacon spoke against that part of the bill which would have prolonged the effectiveness of the embargo. Story's speech approved the initial enactment of the embargo but questioned the wisdom of any act which would raise the possibility of the continuation of it for any great length of time. Further, in early January Story began an attack on the administration's determination not to increase naval preparedness. On January 4, he introduced a resolution that the ad hoc committee on military and naval preparedness "be instructed to inquire into the expediency of increasing our Naval Establishment." He informed his colleagues that if war was to be the result of their deliberations, he was decidedly in favor of fighting on the ocean, and he offered his resolution to encourage discussion on the propriety of augmenting the naval force. The resolution was never considered.[7] Instead, on January 10, 1809, the House carried the Senate bill to increase the naval force by a vote of 64 to 59. On January 16, 1809, it reversed itself and sent the bill to a joint conference committee by a vote of 68 to 55. On January 18, the reversal was upheld by a vote of 67 to 53. Bacon and Story both favored the Senate bill and voted together each time. At the same time, however, Bacon and Story voted against two bills introduced by Federalists, first to remove Chittenden's motion (November 13, 1808) for the repeal of the em-

bargo from the table and then to enact the bill. In other words, although they had spoken on December 29 for repeal of the embargo
at some not too distant date, both Story and Bacon refused to consent to an immediate repeal on January 4.[8]

The disunity among Republicans on the naval bills soon spread
rapidly to other issues as well. In the debate following the naval
establishment bill on whether to have a special session of Congress,
Federalist Josiah Quincy of Massachusetts called the extra session a
design by the majority "to soothe the people, impatient under the
embargo, until the spring elections are passed." Virginians John W.
Eppes and John G. Jackson rose to the occasion and bitterly attacked Quincy's partisanship, but Ezekiel Bacon made by far the
most significant speech on convening the special session of Congress. Bacon accused Quincy of disturbing the "state of much apparent tranquillity" which had characterized the debate on the naval
bill. He further accused Quincy of fearing "that this state of things
might conduct us and the nation to some happy result" and, to prevent such an occurrence, of reviving party spirit "to excite agitation
in the House, and alarm, division, and discord among the people."
The time had come, said Bacon, for the majority to answer Quincy's
question of when the embargo should be abandoned and what measures should be adopted in its place. Bacon favored some form of
nonintercourse with Great Britain and France or "some other measure as a substitute upon its [the embargo's] removal." If no one else
would propose such a measure, he "would feel no hesitation in offering it [the motion] at an early day, and placing the time of it at no
very distant period." There were many reasons to adopt such a
course, but Bacon said he would do it if for no other reason than to
protect

> the feelings of that portion of our citizens who by such addresses to their
> passions and their prejudices as we yesterday heard from my colleague
> [Quincy] have been induced to believe that this was a system of perpet-
> ual exclusion from the ocean, and a permanent abandonment of com-
> mercial enterprise. . . . In the furtherance of this desirable object, I
> have reason to believe that a large majority of the House will unite, and
> having done this will consent to do no more. Let the crisis come when it
> will, it is our duty to meet it; let its consequences rest upon those by
> whose representations and instigations it has been promoted and
> encouraged.[9]

This speech signified an important change in Bacon's thinking that went far beyond a fear of Federalist victories in New England's elections. Writing to Story to explain his speech against Quincy, Bacon said he still felt the same antipathy for Quincy and the Federalists as he had when Story was in Washington, but increasingly he also found himself opposed to the plans of the majority of his own party. Whereas other members of the majority had attacked Quincy in words "probably rather more personal than was politic," Bacon tried to avoid personal attacks and speak "in the style of solemn Expostulation"—a plan "better calculated for the temper of our quarter of the Country." The central theme of his letter to Story was that the Southern Republicans were "willing to support our commercial rights by the present system or by War as we shall think best, but . . . [would] never consent to take nonintercourse & nonimportation as a substitute for the Embargo." Bacon theorized that a stalemate had developed between the commercial Northeast and the agrarian South and West—New England would bear neither a prolonged embargo nor war, and the other parts of the Union would not support commercial rights in any other way:

> The Result in my opinion is that the rights of Commerce will be abandoned by the Nation, that the Southern Section will never again be induced to risque any thing essential for them, & that New England may thank her own fortunes for the ruin which in my View impends over her best Interests. —This is a gloomy Future, but I am more & more convinced that it will soon be realized, the Events & Conversations of the last three Days [regarding the bill to have an extra session of Congress in May] particularly confirm me in it.[10]

During the first week in February, Bacon again wrote to Story that his conduct and that of the other Northeastern Republicans had been severely criticized by the majority, but on February 25, 1809, Bacon triumphantly reported to his friend and former colleague that the Northern section had beaten away all attempts by the Southern section to add any type of war measure to the nonintercourse and nonimportation bills. The Northern section "held their majority on almost every question, . . . and the fact is (between ourselves & it must go no further) the administration have been completely beaten in the house, by the Northern Interest," of which the Federalists comprised only about twenty-five.[11]

In summary, Jefferson's fears that Bacon had been converted to Federalism (Table 7.2) and Spivak's conclusion that a fear of Federalist political opposition in the North determined Bacon's opposition to the embargo overlook the importance to Bacon of significant ideological differences between Northern and Southern Republicans. These disagreements began over the issue of use of the navy in asserting America's rights to trade and were exacerbated during debates over the question of using extreme commercial restrictions or warlike measures to assert these rights. Table 7.3 tests the sincerity of Bacon's argument by charting those Republicans who voted in the extreme positions on the naval and embargo repeal votes. If Bacon's letters accurately state his position, one would expect those who favored the naval issue in the extreme to vote similarly on bills for repealing the embargo.

Table 7.3
**Republican Extremists, Navy and Post-Feb. 13 Scales:
Tenth House, Second Session**

Legislator	State	Navy	2/13	Legislator	State	Navy	2/13
Bacon	Ma	+	+	Van Horne	Md	+	+
Ilsley	Ma	+	+	Montgomery	Md	+	×
Storer	Ma	+	+	Smith, S.	Pa	×	+
Durell	NH	+	+	Southard	NJ	×	+
Shaw	VT	+	×	Boyd	NJ	×	+
Sloan	NJ	+	+	Lyon	Ky	+	+
Riker	NY	+	+	Dawson	Va	+	×
Mumford	NY	+	+	Holmes	Va	+	×
Van Alen	NY	+	+	Troup	Ga	+	×
Van Cortlandt	NY	+	+	Love	Va	+	×
Swart	NY	+	+	Newton	Va	+	×

+ = Extremely favorable
× = Extremely unfavorable

For Bacon and three other New England Republicans, the naval issue was "predictive" of an extreme position on the embargo's repeal, but their positions must be weighed against one (Lemuel Shaw) who was at the opposite end of the spectrum on the repeal of the embargo issue. Thus, it may be said that 80 percent of those who were extremely in favor of naval preparedness linked this issue with the necessity of repealing the embargo. In the Middle states, the percentage is nearly as high (64 percent), but in the Southern and Western states only one Republican strongly favored *both* issues (17 percent). Overall, of those who appeared in the extreme positions on both scales, Northerners clearly predominated.[12]

Two conclusions may be drawn from Table 7.3. First, because so few Republicans voted in the extreme positions on both issues, some other factor must have been responsible for the embargo's repeal (see ensuing discussion). In other words, Ezekiel Bacon could not, by himself, have caused a "revolution." Second, although very few may have followed Bacon's thinking, Table 7.3 does support his position that Northern and Southern Republicans were at opposite ends of the spectrum on more issues than simply a continuation of the embargo. This same concern is repeated in a speech that Bacon gave more than a year later. Whether peace could long continue under the outrageous attacks by European nations (chiefly Great Britain), Bacon argued, was "a question of dark and doubtful solution." Only "intuitive statesmen, who can discern nothing but plain sailing and serene skies over the political ocean of the times" would dare to convert "civil institutions . . . more happily adapted to diffuse the blessings of peace . . . to wield the scourge of distant war." Yet there were also those seeking equally simplistic answers who would "[throw] ourselves upon the magnanimity and forebearance of Great Britain." Either policy, Bacon warned, "[could] only be dangerous to listen to, and ruinous to adopt."

For the nation, Bacon asserted, the embargo was "a noble and severe sacrifice on the part of its agricultural interest [the South and West], for the vindication of its commercial interest." Unfortunately, the sacrifice had been "too generally repaid with the most arrogant ingratitude and folly [by New Englanders]." But Bacon also asserted that "the enjoyment of a free and unrestrained commerce with the world is, in the nature of things, our indefeasible right." Given these two diametrically opposed "factions," therefore, Bacon felt that the greatest danger the nation faced was the temptation "to think that the path, which leads out of all our embarassments, is plain, easy and obvious." What Bacon favored was "a fixed and habitual system of peace, tranquility and public economy" that would unite the nation through a system of internal improvements that sounds very much like the American System of the 1820s. That more money had not been invested in such a system that would truly unify the nation "by directing our energies to pursuits conformable to our natural situation, . . . to the accomplishment of which . . . are in our own hands" was attributable directly to "the perplexing hostility of party animosity [the Federalists], and . . . the narrow views of local policy [the Southern Republicans]."[13]

If Bacon's speech and his letters and statements during the second session accurately reflect the situation of the Congress, it is little wonder that the naval issue so disrupted Republican party unity. Northern Republicans looked for a middle road between commercial restriction and war or submission, and linked the naval and embargo issues in order to frustrate both the Southern "war hawks" and the pro-British Federalists. Only after the embargo was removed could peaceful means be pursued for solving the nation's long-term economic ills (half of Bacon's July 4, 1810 speech was devoted to a comparison of Federalist and Republican monetary policies) and expose the "misguided [Federalist] party animosity, by which our national energies have been wasted, and our arm of defence palsied and unnerved."[14]

What cannot be so easily documented, however, is Bacon's assertion that Southerners favored war as a replacement for the embargo. In fact, voting in the session reveals no such unified position. It is true that Southerners more than any other group opposed the repeal of the embargo (Table 7.4), but it is also true that an almost equal number of Southerners could not decide between continued embargo and more vigorous actions.

Table 7.4
Republican Divisions by Section, Post-Feb. 13 Scale:
Tenth House, Second Session

	New England		Middle States		South & West	
	Number	Percent	Number	Percent	Number	Percent
Pro-Embargo Repeal	6	43	10	32	1	2
Moderate	5	36	11	35	17	44
Anti-Embargo Repeal	3	21	10	32	21	54
Totals	14	100	31	99	39	100

As Table 7.4 indicates, those who intensely opposed repealing the embargo outnumbered those strongly in favor of discarding it by a two-to-one majority (34 to 17). Unfortunately for the former group, however, what finally decided the issue in favor of repeal were the 33 moderate Republicans whose votes eventually carried the day, and of these a majority were Southerners (Table 7.5).[15]

Table 7.5
Republican Moderates, Post-Feb. 13 Scale:
Tenth House, Second Session

Legislator	State	Legislator	State
Fisk	Vt	Smith, J.	Va
Smith, J. K.	NH	Burwell	Va
Cutts	Ma	Gholson	Va
Green	Ma	Goodwyn	Va
Wilbour	RI	Nicholas	Va
		Morrow, John	Va
Hiester	Pa	Wilson	Va
Findley	Pa	Dawson	Va
Richards	Pa	Williams	SC
Pugh	Pa	Marion	SC
Boyd	NJ	Moore, T.	SC
Helms	NJ	Alston, W.	NC
Lambert	NJ	Alexander	NC
Newbold	NJ	Sawyer	NC
Moore, N. R.	Md	Blackledge	NC
Humphrey	NY	Bibb	Ga
Verplanck	NY	Morrow, Jeremiah	Oh

The speeches of many of those Southerners identified in Table 7.5 attest to their role as moderates in the session and as the group responsible for the embargo's final repeal. Willis Alston of North Carolina said he voted to repeal the embargo only after he saw that there were others who "believed the nation looked forward to a modification of the embargo." Although he favored continuing the embargo, he nevertheless agreed with the new majority that a nonintercourse system would be the best measure to adopt in its place, leaving the question of war to the first session of the Eleventh Congress. William A. Burwell of Virginia said he had always expected a lifting of the embargo in the spring or summer, and he would support whatever course the majority would favor. Furthermore, he was totally opposed to war at the present time. He wanted to give the belligerents one more opportunity to avoid war. Wilson Cary Nicholas, the initiator of the January 24 bill to follow a repeal of the embargo with letters of marque and reprisal, compromised in the end with the language of the nonintercourse system. Speaking perhaps for many of his colleagues whose names appear in Table 7.5, Nicholas cited his reason for favoring nonintercourse: "If it were my individual concern, I should certainly rely upon my own judgment: but when everything dear to my country is at stake, I cannot justify to myself a pertinacious adherence to a proposition already rejected by a great majority, which would hazard the loss of a measure, the best, in my opinion, that can be attained." Even Virginian John W. Eppes, who scales as an extremist opposed to the embargo's repeal and was one of the loudest members of the majority in advocating a war or embargo alternative, stated that when the majority of the House determined to overrule his opinion, he felt he had to acquiesce. Citing the unprepared state of the nation to conduct a war, Eppes declared himself "willing to take this one chance of peace, and for that reason I am willing to postpone the period of issuing letters of marque and reprisal, till the first of June."[16]

As with Bacon's change in voting behavior, it is instructive in understanding the thinking of these moderate Republicans to look at voting on the naval issue. For Bacon and other Northern Republicans, the naval issue served as a middle ground between war and continued embargo. As Table 7.3 indicates, however, few Southerners were attracted to the Northern position. Only Matthew Lyon of Kentucky supported strongly both an expanded navy and the embargo's repeal.[17] The other Southern Republicans who were intensely pronavy were probably motivated more by the needs of the districts they represented than by any attempt to use the naval issue to build a moderate consensus to which their colleagues could rally. John Love wrote at least one letter in late December recommending a constituent for naval service due to the "expected increase of our navy establishment," and Thomas Newton wrote at least three similar letters from late December through early February.[18] Indeed, Newton, who represented Norfolk, often spoke in the House in the years preceding the War of 1812 regarding the unprepared state of his district for war. Contemporaneous with the naval debate, on December 26, 1808, Newton revealed his feelings most honestly in a letter to Virginia Governor John Tyler, Sr., asking the governor to defend Norfolk and Portsmouth "against the annoyance of an enemy." Congress would do little, he said, and he was "persuaded that the subject deserves attention, as it is uncertain how long we shall remain in a state of peace, if such a state of things as the present, can be called peace."[19]

Although Newton and the other Republicans in Table 7.3 voted with Northerners who wanted to increase the naval establishment, he and the others aside from Lyon vigorously opposed the repeal of the embargo. What seemed at the first of the session to be good strategy for the majority party to follow, "three alternatives alone . . . to be chosen from. 1. embargo. 2. war. 3. submission and tribute," broke down under the pressure of the Northern Republicans.[20] Simply put, the administration had no contingency plans for such an occurrence, and the general assumption, confirmed by reading the letters of Jefferson, Gallatin, and Madison, that *some* consensus would emerge between war and embargo as the session progressed proved faulty.[21] In the face of Bacon's "Northern position" Southerners fragmented, and the embargo's fate was sealed.

Reginald C. Stuart has recently offered an interpretation of voting in the closing days of the second session of the Tenth Congress that differs substantially from the account given above. Whereas our focus has been on the Northern Republicans' naval strategy, Stuart isolates 32 Republicans, defined as "militants," who supported limited reprisals against Great Britain. The core members of this group were Southerners closely allied (and, in the case of John G. Jackson, related) to president-elect Madison and Treasury Secretary Gallatin. These men, by taking a militant stand against Great Britain instead of "marking time" by following nonintercourse, "took the first major step on the road to the War of 1812."[22]

What Stuart's analysis fails to specify, however, is how these militants led the Congress into a war stance in 1812. As with prior students of the war's origins, Stuart adopts a multicausal approach to why war came when it did that ignores the formative role of a "militant" carry-over group of congressmen from the second session of the Tenth Congress. "More time, continued British arrogance, further exasperation over diplomacy, further affronts to neutrals' rights and national honor, and a shift in the composition of the House," Stuart concludes, "were all required to erode the strength of the conservative bloc of the Republican party, which held the balance of power between the militants and the Federalists in 1809."[23]

It is the final argument of this chapter that the naval issue, which

Stuart overlooks, as have the others who have studied this problem, provides a behavioral link between the repeal of the embargo in 1809 and the movement to war in 1812. The naval issue also helps to clarify the precise contribution of the War Hawks, most of whom were Republicans from the southeastern seaboard states, to the Congress's deliberations in the war session of the Twelfth Congress.

During the second session of the Eleventh Congress, Virginian William A. Burwell introduced a bill (January 19, 1810) that would have armed American merchant vessels and provided a system of government convoys to protect American shipping. Burwell claimed that his bill was a plan to prevent war from occurring and was strictly a defensive measure to ensure national honor and independence. He declared himself "decidedly against war" but "equally confirmed in the opinion that the time had arrived when it became the duty of the United States to maintain by force, if necessary, their right to carry on commerce to every country which will receive it on fair and honorable terms." Burwell introduced his motion, he said, "to obtain a decision of the House, whether they would employ our naval force to convoy our trade to those nations not having in force decrees against our commerce, and whether they would permit associations among our merchants for the purpose of arming and defending themselves in their trade to any foreign nation."[24]

Burwell's motion was referred to a select committee which issued its report on February 9. A debate was scheduled for February 26, but the issue became subsumed in debate on the Senate refusal to accept the first commercial bill offered in the session (Macon's Bill #1), and the Committee of the Whole began its debate of the combined bills on March 5, 1810. Burwell favored the bill as a means of "defending the strictly neutral commerce of the United States." John W. Eppes said he believed the bill would allow commerce to "resume its natural channel, [so] that our farmers and planters might send a part of their produce to Portugal, Spain, Germany, and Holland." But the committee eventually recalled its motion, and the measure was dropped in the House. When the Senate amended Macon's Bill #2 by adding a convoy system, the House refused to concur with the Senate action.[25]

In the third session, Gurdon S. Mumford of New York introduced a motion late in the session (February 28, 1811) "that a committee be appointed to inquire into the expediency of authorizing, by law, merchant vessels of the United States to arm in defence of their persons and property on the high seas, against the spoilations of all or any of the belligerents."[26] The motion never received an answer, however, because of the lateness of the session.

Federalists, in the period following the repeal of the embargo, used the naval issue to confuse the Republicans. Early in the first session of the Eleventh Congress, Connecticut Federalist Samuel W. Dana introduced a bill for arming American commerce in an attempt to distinguish between "resistance to aggression of foreign nations, and the principle of reprisal." On May 30, 1809, Dana invited his colleagues to "transfer to the water that system which exists on the land, for a practical demonstration of which he would refer to gentlemen from the western country, where he understood that citizens, individually or combined, armed for their defence against predatory incursions or attack." His system, Dana affirmed, was directed against only one principle—blockade by proclamation as practiced by both the French and the British. His motion was tabled and never reached the floor.[27]

In the second session, however, when Burwell offered his February 28 motion, Dana and other Federalists refused to rush blindly into the scheme. Dana asked Burwell how many and what types of ships would be used in the convoy operation. He feared that the bill was a party measure designed not to protect neutral shipping but rather to ensure a battle "between one of our vessels and a vessel of one of the belligerents, and thus involve us in war." Josiah Quincy also suggested that the committee rise and consider its proposal more carefully. If the bill "was seriously meant to be passed, if it was not merely a newspaper measure, or party hocus pocus, not only its principle but its details must be rigidly examined."[28]

Therefore, questions of whether to expand the naval establishment in order that it might be used to convoy American merchant ships, or more effectively protect the nation's coastal towns, or to allow merchant ships to arm in self-defense, remained as sensitive and emotionally charged in the Eleventh Congress as they had in the second session of the Tenth Congress. In each instance that the issue arose between 1809 and December of 1811, a majority of the Republican congressmen were reluctant to support such measures due to their aversion to large navies and the large amounts of public expenditures necessary to finance an extensive naval establishment. Defections from the majority view occurred primarily among representatives from coastal states who either feared an attack on their unprotected shorelines or who sought relief for their merchantmen. Federalists were also divided in sentiment between those who favored a forcible defense of neutral rights and those who feared that armed vessels might lead to war with Great Britain or be used to enforce nonintercourse or embargoes. As the Republicans began to voice an inclination to go to war with Britain, even Dana carefully reassessed his position so as to preclude the possibility of armed merchantmen and convoys being used as justification for a declaration of war.

During the early debates of the war session of the Twelfth Congress, however, the situation changed dramatically. As one of the first, major items of business, South Carolinian Langdon Cheves reported a naval bill designed to force the majority party to recognize the importance to all parts of the nation of a naval force capable of protecting commerce. The United States was destined, the report stated, to be a great naval power without an inordinate expenditure of funds.[29] On January 17, 1812, Cheves gave the reasoning behind his committee's recommendations. A respectable naval establishment, he said, was "the only effectual means of causing our commercial rights to be respected." Although he expected few men to disagree with such a statement, Cheves challenged those who opposed the naval bill to reflect that a strong naval force would be cheaper than a land army. Furthermore, twelve "seventy-fours" and twenty frigates (the number in the bill) would be sufficient to protect the nation in its coastal waters and "defend our ports and harbors against the naval power of Great Britain." In short, the commercial and agricultural interests of the nation as well as the protection it would provide required the national government to construct such a naval force.

In addition to these arguments, however, much of Cheves's speech was devoted to convincing the members of the majority party of the necessity of changing their old ways:

> I know . . . how many and how strong are the prejudices, how numerous and how deeply laid are the errors which I have to encounter in the discussion of this question. . . . I have been told that this subject is unpopular, and it has been not indistinctly hinted, that those who become the zealous advocates of the bill will not advance by their exertions the personal estimation in which they may be held by their political

associates. . . . I wish to lead no man, and I am determined not to be blindly led by any man. In acting with a party, I do so, because I adopt their leading principles and politics as the best, and because I believe, from the nature of free Government, it is necessary so to act to give efficiency to the exertions of any individual; but I do not feel myself, therefore, bound to renounce my deliberate opinions on all the great interests of the nation, or to take no independent part in the exertions of the party to which I belong.[30]

Simply put, in order to declare war against the British, Republicans would have to learn to think in different ways from the past.

Supporters of a strong naval establishment used most of the arguments presented by Cheves. Virginian Burwell Bassett listed three reasons to prefer a navy over an army: 1) navies were less expensive, 2) navies were less dangerous to civil institutions, and 3) the nation was particularly vulnerable to attack by a strong naval power. Samuel L. Mitchill of New York reminded the majority party that the conflict with Great Britain was strictly of a commercial nature. He did not, however, urge that all of the nation's resources should be committed to a naval force—"our nearest and dearest interests are on *terra firma*, and there they should be preserved and maintained." A strong naval force, combined with an army, would allow the nation to fight with all its strength, and not with "one hand tied behind our back." South Carolinian William Lowndes supported a strong navy with the statement that the motive behind Britain's injuries to American shipping was the desire to destroy a commercial rival. It was, therefore, a strange circumstance for him to find that many members of the Republican majority expected to obtain an honorable peace without a naval force. To terminate the war with Great Britain on honorable terms, Lowndes believed that the British would have to believe that their losses would be as great as America's should the war continue. "But when your whole trade—your foreign and your coasting trade, are destroyed, (and without a naval force it seems to me that they must be,) what argument would your most dextrous negotiator employ," he asked, "to show that the loss of England would be equal to your own from the continuance of the war?" Virginian Hugh Nelson tried to persuade his colleagues that a naval force was necessary even if Canada were also captured. The cause of the war was essentially commercial, and whatever gains were made would have to be won on the sea.[31]

Republicans in opposition to Cheves's resolutions contended that a naval establishment was an unnecessary expenditure of public money, played into the hands of the enemy by attacking the British at their strength, and would even alter the nature of republican government. Pennsylvanian Adam Seybert condemned the proposals because a navy would not be able to protect American commerce and because the naval expense would continue far beyond the end of the war. Samuel McKee argued that the permanent taxes necessary to preserve the navy would negate the foundation of republican economy in government. Richard M. Johnson countered arguments that the navy would be less expensive than an army with recollections that the main reason for Republican victory in the elections of 1800 was the system of exorbitant tax measures adopted by the Federalists for the perpetuation of an extensive naval establishment. Pennsylvanians Jonathan Roberts and John Smilie refused to accept the premise of the report's sponsors that the United States was destined to be a great naval power. James Fisk of Vermont and William W. Bibb of Georgia opposed the plans because of the "idiocy" of fighting Great Britain at her strength. They preferred that the nation fight according to its strength and its enemy's weakness. Capturing Nova Scotia and Canada would be the only means of protecting American shipping, according to Fisk. When these objects were accomplished, the British would cease to enter American waters because they would no longer have any colony where her ships could be refitted.[32]

The end result was mixed. Enough Republicans supported appropriations to repair and fit out the existing navy to pass the first sections of Cheves's bill, but beyond this point a majority of the party would not go. The importance of this bill, however, is to be understood only in comparison with voting on the naval issue during the second session of the Tenth Congress (see Table 7.6). In 1809, 75 percent of New England Republicans were pronavy; in 1812 only 33 percent were in the same category. Middle state Republicans evinced a similar decline in support in both the pro and moderate categories (25 to 17 percent in pro and 41 to 21 in moderate). What is most striking, however, is the change in the South and West where pros and moderates *increased* from 17 to 29 and 33 to 39 percent respectively. The significance of these shifts is underscored when one constructs a new table of extreme positions (Table 7.7).[33]

In contrast to the results shown in Table 7.3, which linked the

Table 7.6
The Naval Issue and Republicans:
Tenth House, Second Session and Twelfth House, First Session

| | New England | | | |
| | 1809 | | 1812 | |
	Number	Percent	Number	Percent
Pro-	9	75	4	33
Moderate	3	25	4	33
Anti-	0	0	4	33
Totals	12	100	12	99

| | Middle States | | | |
| | 1809 | | 1812 | |
	Number	Percent	Number	Percent
Pro-	8	25	5	17
Moderate	13	41	6	21
Anti-	11	34	18	62
Totals	32	100	29	100

| | South and West | | | |
| | 1809 | | 1812 | |
	Number	Percent	Number	Percent
Pro-	7	17	12	29
Moderate	14	33	16	39
Anti-	21	50	13	32
Totals	42	100	41	100

navy and the repeal of the embargo, Republicans in the Twelfth
Congress who held extreme positions for both the navy and war
declined in New England and the Middle states (from 80 to 43 percent and 64 to 27 percent, respectively), but increased from 17 to 50
percent for Southerners. Most Republicans, it must be reempha-
sized, continued to hold old attitudes toward the navy and refused to
link naval expansion and war. That is, Republicans in all sections
could still be antinavy and prowar. But by 1812 for many Southern
Republicans—notably Thomas Newton, Willis Alston, Burwell
Bassett, William Blackledge, and John Dawson from the Tenth
Congress and new members like John C. Calhoun, Langdon
Cheves, and William Lowndes who became War Hawks in 1812—*all*
issues had come to be viewed as war issues, irrespective of specific

Table 7.7
Republican Extremists, Favoring the Navy and War:
Twelfth House, First Session

Legislator	State	Navy	War	Legislator	State	Navy	War
Green	Ma	+	+	Alston, W.	NC	+	+
Turner	Ma	+	+	Blackledge	NC	+	+
Widgery	Ma	+	+	Bassett	Va	+	+
Hall, O.	NH	×	+	Newton	Va	+	+
Seaver	Ma	×	+	Pleasants	Va	+	+
Strong	Vt	×	+	Calhoun	SC	+	+
Shaw	Vt	×	+	Cheves	SC	+	+
				Lowndes	SC	+	+
Little	Md	+	+	Dawson	Va	+	+
McKim	Md	+	+	Bibb	Ga	×	+
Wright	Md	+	+	Hall, B.	Ga	×	+
Pond	NY	+	+	Johnson	KY	×	+
Sammons	NY	+	×	McKee	KY	×	+
Tracy	NY	+	×	Desha	KY	×	+
Sage	NY	×	+	Pickens	NC	×	+
Brown	Pa	×	+	Cochran	NC	×	+
Lacock	Pa	×	+	Grundy	Te	×	+
Lyle	Pa	×	+	Rhea	Te	×	+
Morgan	Pa	×	+				
Roberts	Pa	×	+				
Smilie	Pa	×	+				
Anderson	Pa	×	+				
Lefever	Pa	×	+				

+ = Extremely favorable
× = Extremely unfavorable

content or sectional biases.[34] As for Bacon and others who favored peace over war, when the Southern War Hawks took even the naval issue under their wings, there was no middle position left to occupy. Undoubtedly Bacon, who scales as a moderate on both the naval and war issues in the Twelfth Congress, realized this situation as is indicated by his excessive absences late in the session in company with other Republicans who felt the nation was unprepared for war.[35]

Ironically, therefore, the issue that proved to be the most disruptive force in 1809, shattered party unity, and thrust the nation into a situation that in Jefferson's words "[shook] our Union, to it's center" provided the earliest clue in the Twelfth Congress that war would (or could) be declared. Attitudes toward the navy did not cause the shift in Republican voting that made war possible, but rather were a sign that consistent prowar feeling had, at long last, developed among a core of predominately Southern Republicans. And when the war decision came, preceded as it was by a 60-day embargo to clear the seas of American ships, Republican unity was reestablished along the lines envisioned by the administration in November 1808. The failure of the embargo had led, finally, to war.

CHAPTER EIGHT

Rhetoric in Transition

The Emergence of the Diabolism Theme, 1808–1811

Quincy Wright, in his extensive study of war, emphasizes that symbols contribute significantly to the initiation of conflicts between nations. Hostilities, he argues, arise "immediately in the world of symbols, not in the world of conditions." While various material conditions "promote opinions favorable to war," in the final analysis war is "always intentional." Through the symbolic acts of designated leaders, nations indulge in war-justifying interpretations that transcend the strictly objective implications of events and circumstances. Symbols, "usually richer in affective than in informative meaning" and often referring to "fictions, myths, and stereotypes with little relation to conditions," influence "the 'weight of opinion' among those with authority to act for the group" and promote a unity of public opinion within the nation. These effects, Wright notes, are achieved largely by symbols which emphasize the enemy's diabolism and hostility toward the noble ideals of the community. In short, the initiation of war involves the emergence of a richly affective rhetoric of diabolism as one of those "symbolic acts which mean war and justify it" by drawing upon a nation's most fundamental vocabularies of acceptable motives.[1]

Kenneth Burke sheds light on the sources of diabolism's appeal as he discusses the cultural and symbolic functions of victimage rituals. In his words, the " 'guilt' intrinsic to hierarchal order (the only kind of 'organizational' order we have ever known) calls correspondingly for 'redemption' through *victimage*." Such is the effect of "the great religious and theological doctrine that forms the incunabula of our culture." The fundamental logic of our cultural symbol system is such that, "if Order, then guilt; if guilt, then need for redemption; but any such 'payment' is victimage."[2] A people strongly committed to the ideal of peace, but simultaneously faced with the prospect of war, must believe that the fault for any such disruption of their ideal lies with the behavior and evil intentions of others. Hierarchic guilt otherwise would threaten to drive the nation toward some form of self-mortification.[3] Victimage rhetoric in the form of appeals to diabolism resolves this potential difficulty by offering redemption to the nation through the identification of a suitable and plausible scapegoat. Such appeals, generally speaking, characterize the nation's adversary as a savage aggressor driven by irrational desires for conquest and seeking to subjugate innocent victims by force of arms—in short, as a diabolical agent.[4] This image of the adversary as Satan's surrogate presents to the nation a perfect antagonist whose sacrifice justifies the breach of peace as it promises to eliminate the source of trouble. Hence, the symbols of diabolism enable nations to transform conditions of international tension into perceptions of crisis proportions.

This analysis of the role played by the symbols of diabolism is particularly relevant to understanding the course of events leading to the declaration of war in 1812. The peculiar timing and emotional origins of the war have been an object of comment and interest for historians who have noted that there was probably less cause for war in 1812 than in preceding years.[5] The basic controversy with Great Britain dragged on for nearly a decade before war eventually was declared on June 18—ironically just after England repealed the Orders in Council. While slow transatlantic communications prevented Americans from learning of their victory over "the chief symbol of discord" in time to avoid hostilities, the commitment to war was largely a product of hardened attitudes toward the British on the part of a Congress which chose to disregard earlier "omens of concession." The decision to fight, in other words, would have been deferred, or possibly would have come years sooner, had it conformed more nearly to the world of conditions. Instead, less rational forces influenced the nation's collective judgment as differences between the two governments were blown into a major controversy. British insensitivity and preoccupation with the struggle against Napoleon so frustrated the situation that Americans, insisting upon the fullness of their rights, concluded they had no choice other than the humiliation of submission or the tribulations of war.[6]

The governing party's emergence into this realm of highly emotional and abstract symbols occurred gradually.[7] Eventually, the point was reached where the party that thought of itself as the defender of republicanism decided further submissions to British encroachments would undermine its control of the government and thereby discredit republican ideology itself.[8] Defending neutral rights was equated by Republicans with protecting the nation's integrity as a republican polity. When they finally lost faith in schemes of commercial retaliation as a means of preserving maritime rights, they began to believe that war was their only remaining alternative, for submission to the Orders in Council could lead only to the return of colonial status.[9]

This movement away from the policy of economic coercion was justified in the war Congress, as we have seen, by a rhetoric of diabolism.[10] Republican speakers dramatized the theme of recolonization and thereby nationalized the cause for war as they emphasized Britain's intransigence and hostility toward the rights of its chief commercial rival. From the perspective of prowar arguments in 1812, there was no remaining hope of changing the policies or motives of a relentless British government through appeals to its economic interests. The nation's adversary was bent upon its course of commercial monopoly at the expense of American independence. Nothing short of an appeal to arms would convince Great Britain to abstain from further encroachments, and additional delays would only embolden the enemy while weakening the intended victim. The exigencies of the situation, as defined by Republican rhetors, urgently required the nation to act in self-defense against a malevolent enemy who was advancing systematically toward the subjugation of the young republic.

Before the war Congress, however, diabolism remained undeveloped by the majority party as a mechanism for triggering the "imperiled republic" theme in a form that applied to the whole nation, not just to narrow partisans.[11] Following Britain's attack on the *Chesapeake*, Congress agreed to an embargo instead of war, arguing that it would be an effective means of altering hostile policies while protecting the nation's resources from further depletions. Embargo was not a form of submission because it had the potential of improving the nation's position relative to Great Britain. By implication, the British were neither beyond influence nor hopelessly committed to policies that threatened American rights and sovereignty. However, failure to recede in the face of firm resistance by the United States would prove the immutability of Britain's hostility and necessitate an appeal to force. A test of the adversary's motives had been devised, amounting to the proposition that persistence in spite of America's resistance proved Britain's malevolence.

The challenge for those who would advocate war was not to hypothesize evil motives—for suspicions about Britain's true motives were widespread—but to prove that the test for those motives had been administered with unequivocal results. After 1808, Republicans struggled with this problem for three years until their rhetoric evolved by the third session of the Eleventh Congress to the point of establishing British diabolism. The development of Republican prowar rhetoric through this period of transition merits closer examination for the more precise explanation it provides of how symbolic acts contributed to the movement toward war.

As Republicans struggled toward a conclusive interpretation of British intentions, they argued that Britain could be coerced economically into respecting America's commercial rights if only the nation would stand firm. After passing the embargo in December 1807, however, they soon discovered domestic.pressures mounting for its repeal. With nonintercourse replacing embargo in March 1809 and then Macon's Bill #2 reopening trade with the belligerents in May 1810, Republican spokesmen could only lament a series of legislative retreats which, they argued, would leave England with the distinct impression there was no American will to resist further encroachments. As one distressed legislator complained in January of 1810, "[By] tamely submitting to the aggressions of England, we encourage her to carry on her underhand system of war upon us; whereas, if we were to come to a stand and resolve to resist every future attempt, she would cease her piratical practices towards us."[12] Even the radical voice of Joseph Desha, warning that "the very existence of our independence is endangered" by a "rapacious and tyrannical Power," blamed America's failure to resist in large measure for the continuing crisis. In his words, "Sir, my anxious wish is to avert war; but, if we keep receding, we must calculate on additional encroachments; whereas, if we form a manly stand, act with firmness, show Britain that we will not abandon our pretensions, she will recede."[13]

As late as the second session of the Eleventh Congress, that is, the enemy was not represented as bent upon America's subjugation at any price. In fact, the problem was that England's motives still had not been tested adequately by American resolve. In the words of David S. Garland, "All that Great Britain wanted, was to give to our commerce that direction which best comported with her interests, and to impress our seamen at pleasure; and, so long as we will permit her to do that, she has no inducement to negotiate with us." He was persuaded, though, "that if this nation would put her commerce under the protection of the national flag, that Great Britain would not make war upon it for the purpose of enforcing her Orders in Council, and, if she did, the sooner this nation knew it the better."[14] Firm resistance, he argued, must be shown before the nation could know how determined and relentless its adversary really was.

In short, the rhetorical advancement of the case for war had stalled on a crucial point. Without a demonstrated resolve by the United States, the cardinal point of British perseverance remained a missing premise in the logic of diabolism for nearly three years after passage of the embargo. Otherwise, the basic elements of diabolism were at hand by the time Congress adjourned in 1810. These elements included an ascribed motive of hostility toward American independence, an emergent arrangement of individual events and confrontations around the integrating theme of Britain's hostile motives, and the use of power metaphors to emphasize Britain's reliance on brute force to achieve its goals.

Among those who had participated up to this point in developing the emergent rhetoric of diabolism was Richard M. Johnson, who told his congressional colleagues in November of 1808 that war was the only alternative if the embargo should fail to coerce the English. The object of France, he said, was merely "to destroy our neutrality and involve us in the convulsing wars of Europe," but the object of Great Britain was "a monopoly of our commerce, and the destruction of our freedom and independence." To establish his point, Johnson "retraced" a series of events which "pressed upon us" and clearly "required the arm of [Britain's] Government." However, he added, if the United States would "rigidly enforce" its embargo, his confidence was undiminished that Britain's injustice toward America would be relaxed.[15]

Two days later, John G. Jackson of Virginia, Madison's brother-in-law, ratified Johnson's analysis of British motives while applying the same strategy of organization to establish his point. In Jackson's words:

> We know that it is the wish of the belligerents, who have swallowed up in the vortex of their interminable disputes all the nations of the world but the United States, to unite us in their cause. Each one wishes to form more intimate connexion with us than those we have with its enemy. This disposition is natural; for when we look into private life, we see individuals endeavoring to enlist those who have no concern in the dispute among their partisans in their personal contests. Besides this wish, common to both the belligerents, a spirit of monopoly and jealousy of our commercial greatness has seized upon the Government and people of one of them. It is evident from the conduct of Great Britain for many years past that she cannot consent to submit to the idea that the United States shall be reaping the rich harvest of their neutrality, while her thousand ships are scouring every sea and driving everything from its surface. The commercial spirit of the people of the United States has been the cause of that jealousy.

Accordingly, Jackson's thesis led him next to review the conduct of the British government over the course of the last several years and then to conclude that "all those acts which I have recited [manifest] a determination on the part of Great Britain that our pride shall be humbled, the commerce which we have enjoyed shall be destroyed; that we shall bow to the supremacy of her thousand ships, and that we shall not sail on the ocean without her permission." In short, "the law of nations has been trampled under foot by Great Britain." In his judgment, "The successful invasion of France or the decapitation of the despot of Europe would not to the British Ministry and its friends be a more desirable event than the overthrow of the Republican party in the United States." Despite the dangerous tendencies of "the shark of the ocean," Jackson believed that the "time is not yet come for us to make a sally. It is due to the spirit of this people that every effort should first be made to preserve peace," for once "convinced that everything has been done that can be done, the people will rally around us as one man." In the meantime, he was for strengthening the embargo or even turning to stronger measures short of war to test British resolve.[16]

In February 1809, Joseph Desha of Kentucky conveyed the image of Britain's conduct and motives in a circular letter replete with metaphors of unmitigated power. Referring to "the fangs of despotism" and "the voracious jaws of the monster of the deep," Desha complained that "Britain unprovoked, has outstripped the piracy and perfidy of barbarism. Grasping at universal monopoly, she abandons moral and religious principles, tramples on sacred faith, sports with national law, and arrogantly demands tributary exactions calculated to bring us into a state of bankruptcy, and render us abject vassals instead of a sovereign and free people."[17] But, as John Rhea wrote to his constituents in Tennessee, "Ten millions free sovereign people will never bend the knee of servility to any foreign power."[18] Clearly, the language of diabolism available to members of the Tenth Congress enabled them to focus attention on Britain's hostile intentions, but it did not establish the immutability of those motives. Having retreated from embargo to the weaker measure of nonintercourse, the Tenth Congress left to its successor the unsolved problem of determining how to establish the fixity of British hostility when domestic pressures militated against firm adherence to the policy of commercial resistance.

Republicans in the Eleventh Congress recognized the problem with which they were faced: the initiative still belonged to America's adversaries. The nation had yet to take a stand, and as Andrew Gregg concluded in December 1809,

> On the great question of peace or war it is not easy to form an opinion. There is a great diversity of sentiment in Congress. Some ardent spirits are for immediate war; others, and I believe they are the majority, are in favor of procrastination. I think therefore I may be correct in saying, that it is not probable we will strike the first blow. The door for an adjustment of our differences by negociation will be kept open, should our adversaries be disposed to settle them in that way: but if they are determined on war, I expect they will be resisted by a spirit becoming such a nation as ours."[19]

The problem for Republicans was one of determining whether America's principal adversary was in fact "determined on war."

The state of the diabolism theme as Republicans began their work in the crucial Eleventh Congress was represented well by the ambiguity of Desha's metaphors when he warned of the British threat but recommended a steady adherence to nonintercourse. On the one hand, he argued that this was an "eventful crisis," a time "when not only our most important and inherent rights are about to be wrested from our hands, but when the very existence of our independence is endangered." While France had injured the United States, it was "as a mite to a mountain, compared to the injuries we have received from Britain, our inveterate, rapacious, and relentless enemy." Britain's aggressions against the United States were without a parallel "even in the times of barbarism." Drawing upon these images of Britain forcing its will upon America, Desha easily concluded that the enemy had harbored "a systematic hostility ever since America obtained her independence." Yet, on the other hand, even Desha's language was moderated by accompanying metaphors of seduction as he referred to Britain's "insidious machinations." Although it was a government that "in all cases substitutes power in place of right" and that had "never pardoned our independence," Desha believed the British would try to "obtain, by their insidious arts, what they were not able to retain by arms." While "our passive disposition" would occasion "still greater enormities," a firm adherence to a rigidly enforced nonintercourse would prove sufficiently coercive to protect America's rights from further attacks.[20]

This sort of ambiguity displayed in the language of Republicans made it that much more difficult to justify measures which required a major sacrifice by Americans while promising in return only to fend off a foe who might well be only bluffing. William Bibb put his finger on the problem still facing those who would advocate war when he reminded his colleagues in the House of Representatives that under "our form of Government" the people must be convinced "that an appeal to arms is indispensable for the preservation of their rights." Otherwise, "the prosecution of a successful war" was infeasible. Further, Bibb undercut the case for British diabolism by arguing that every member of Congress knew America's disputes had grown out of the present wars in Europe and that those disputes would "necessarily cease with the war." As he put the matter, "I consider the apprehension of hostility on the part of England entirely visionary, and out of all rational calculation." Why then should nonintercourse be continued, he asked, when all it accomplished was to give "England a monopoly of the commerce of the world"? While no solution was without its disadvantages, the people had no reason to fear an attack on their independence from a beleaguered foe "pressed by the Continental Powers." The Congress should pursue a "practicable course which promises the most advantages" and allows the nation to continue "the enjoyment of peace and plenty."[21] The stage was set, rhetorically at least, for a transition to the logic of Macon's Bill #2.

In March 1810, while explaining the basis of his support for amendments to Macon's Bill #1, John Taylor advanced the logic espoused two months earlier by Bibb. "The non-intercourse law," he said, "is spoken of as a shield from danger, as a cloak to cover us from shame and dishonor; . . . but, as soon as I examine the thing . . . I find that all this mighty resistance, this honorable defence against the belligerents, 'melts into air, thin air.' " The nonintercourse law could not be considered an act of resistance to the Orders in Council when in fact it left Britain with a virtual monopoly of world commerce. Although Thomas Gholson replied that a repeal of nonintercourse "will stamp indelibly upon this Government the characteristics of want of firmness," Taylor underscored the weakness of the previous approach for testing Britain's true intentions. The policy of commercial resistance simply asked for too great a sacrifice by some Americans without establishing the existence of a fundamental threat to the welfare of all Americans. At least, argued Taylor, "If a coercive measure is to be adopted and maintained, for God's sake, let it be a general one, and do not let the whole burden of it be imposed on the tobacco and cotton planter. . . . If there must be resistance, let us have a common stock, and not impose the burden of it exclusively on the two classes I have mentioned."[22] Better yet, he argued a few days later, would be a system that nursed the energy and resources of the nation until the day arrived when Americans were faced by a real threat to their independence: "When the leagued blood-hounds of Europe—leagued by mutual consent in a crusade against republicanism, or more probably united by conquest into one huge monster—shall assail our last asylum of liberty, then will the undivided affections of our people to its Government . . . stand you, or whosoever shall administer our Government, in good stead."[23] Until there was some clearer indication of an imminent attack on the nation, the majority party lacked the triggering mechanism it needed to call out the nation in defense of republicanism, and a diluted effort to resist British encroachments had failed to test adequately Britain's resolve in its campaign against American independence.

Taylor emphasized the failure of the policy of economic coercion and recommended Macon's Bill #2 on the grounds that it provided a new way of testing British perseverance, a means of testing the fixity of hostile intentions without relying upon an impractical mode of active resistance. As he explained to his colleagues in the House:

> The commercial war we have waged against both has been extremely inconvenient to ourselves, without attaining the ultimate end with either of the belligerents. We have made an experiment of this plan of fighting both nations—it won't do. Both the nations with whom we are contending know very well—every member of this House knows, we are overmatched in this contest with both nations; with all the world in fact. Why shall we, from vain pride and from unyielding obstinacy, continue our fruitless exertions against both? I say the policy of this section [of the bill] is more rational and equally honorable for our nation.
>
> In this we may be considered to say, to France and Great Britain— 'We cannot fight you both, we will go on doing the best we can, we will not restrain the industry and enterprise of our citizens, which will be furthering your policy, but we are not the less indignant at the injuries we have received; and if one or the other of you will stand by and see fair play, we will fight the other in the way that suits ourselves. While you are both hostile to us we will have nothing to do with your quarrels; but do us justice and show us the respect we deserve as an independent nation, and then, when there shall be but one foe, we will contend.'[24]

Adopting this logic, the Eleventh Congress managed to retreat further from the old test of British motives without discarding the basic formula that had emerged from the deliberations of the Tenth Congress. It was still the case that if Britain persisted in its hostile policies despite a show of American resistance, there could be no remaining doubt about the finality of its intentions to recolonize a commercial rival. The difference amounted to adopting a new way of drawing the line the enemy had to cross in order to demonstrate its malevolence. Rather than forcing the issue, the United States now would let each belligerent take the initiative either to (a) show respect for American rights by removing restrictive decrees and orders, or (b) prove evil intentions by holding fast to restrictive measures even should the other antagonist choose to respect America's commercial rights. America now had assumed a thoroughly passive mode of resistance to test the enemy's intentions and no longer had to depend upon the impractical expectation of sacrifice by its own commercial interest groups in order to advance toward its ultimate conclusion the case for war.

The very passivity of this new mode of resistance, however,

created new problems by depending upon one of the belligerents to take the bait now being offered. In the meantime, frustrated members of Congress could only lament that America had chosen to cower before the British lion rather than take the manly stand that would cause its enemy to retreat.[25] Yet to muster support for a policy of firm resistance, which in turn required major sacrifices from commercial interest groups, there needed to be prior evidence of the very diabolism that the policy was supposed either to reveal or disprove. At least the United States might now be able to choose its enemy if, as could be expected, the arrogant and powerful shark of the ocean continued to attack its intended victim after Napoleon changed his policies.[26] After all, in the words of Andrew Gregg, Great Britain must be considered "the enemy of my choice" for "she was the first and greatest aggressor, and her injuries towards us have been continued thro almost an uninterrupted succession."[27] Without the cooperation of Britain's chief adversary, though, Republicans could not have advanced further toward a full-fledged, war-justifying rhetoric of diabolism—unless, of course, they had invented still another mode of resistance to test British resolve.

When the opportunistic Napoleon obliged the Americans with an ambiguous gesture toward revocation of his Decrees, Madison was able to proclaim on November 2, 1810, that one of the two belligerents had met the requirements of Macon's Bill #2. The British government, Madison reported on December 5, showed no intention of relinquishing its Orders in Council. By the terms of its own legislation, Congress was committed to cease importations of British goods and to pursue a free intercourse with France. As Ezekiel Bacon had written to Joseph Story on October 22, 1810, following news of the conditional repeal of the French Decrees, "A *resort to arms* must as you suggest be the ultimate result of a perseverance by G. Britain in her orders in Council."[28] The president's report hastened Republicans toward the conclusion that Britain would in fact persevere.

Republicans in the third session of the Eleventh Congress seized upon this turn of events to proclaim that England was revealed as America's true enemy. Langdon Cheves had "never been satisfied of the wisdom or propriety of the law of May last in any other view than one." And that one view was that it "would precipitate us on a particular enemy" because it offered a clear test of the adversaries' true motives.[29] France passed the test by demonstrating, according to presidential proclamation, a willingness to respect the rights of the nation. By its inaction, Great Britain failed the test and demonstrated an intention to persist in its mercantile cupidity at the expense of American sovereignty. A means had been devised for resolving the issue of British motives. The United States had made a "conciliatory" gesture; France "preferred a friendly and amicable intercourse"; England continued to violate "the neutral rights of the United States"; and, as John Rhea concluded, "Great Britain has itself only to blame for the state of things that will be, that is, for the non-intercourse and the events consequent thereto."[30]

The importance of this test of British intentions was reflected in the persistent and sometimes specious attempts of belligerent Republicans to defend the accuracy of Madison's proclamation. In spite of the many reasons to doubt the sincerity of Napoleon's order to revoke his Decrees, and the several reminders to that effect by opposition speakers, it was argued that they were rescinded in fact by the very force of the Emperor's declaration. Cheves claimed that "the declaration of his will is complete evidence of what shall be considered as obligatory on that country. . . . If our rights are now violated, it is a violation independent of the decrees."[31] Rallying behind the president, the veteran Republican Robert Wright reminded his colleagues of the well-known "rapacity of the tyrant of the ocean" and declared that the time had arrived for the country to ignore Great Britain's apologists and "able advocates on this floor." This was no time for America to violate its "national faith" and again recede in the face of a British challenge.[32] It mattered little whether Napoleon was sincere. He had offered Republicans the justification they needed for war with Great Britain.[33]

By choosing to treat the questionable revocation of the French Decrees as a test of British motives, Republicans were able to argue that both adequate cause for war and a case for British culpability had been established. It was no longer a question of blaming the United States for inadequate resolve. Britain's excuse for violating neutral rights had been removed, but the policy of abuse remained unchanged. With the establishment of these premises, the period of rhetorical transition came to a close, and Republicans began to consolidate their forces for the final drive toward a declaration of war.

Cheves had said in February of 1811 that "when the exigencies and necessity of the nation should call for it," Congress would have to apply "the proper excitements" for the country "to meet all its foes, to call forth all its energies." In his opinion, the time was "not far distant" when the government would call upon the people to "resist the injuries inflicted on us."[34] When that call came only nine months later, Republicans capitalized upon the achievements of their colleagues in the Tenth and Eleventh congresses by dramatizing the urgency of defending America against the demon of British usurpations. Although circumstances would have allowed for a different interpretation of Great Britain's motives, Republicans were biased toward a vision of British intransigence by the metaphor of force which had dominated their characterizations of the adversary's conduct. From the beginning of their deliberations over war, Republicans in the Tenth and Eleventh as well as Twelfth congresses turned increasingly to the language of power and physical confrontation as they recounted a series of British "depredations," all the while planting the seeds of an idea which grew into the logic of war. Not surprisingly, President Madison's war message reflected these developments to the point of, as Roger Brown has noted, putting "the worst possible construction on British policies and motives without mentioning settlements, the shifting course of negotiation, and possible alternative interpretations of British intentions. . . . Thus, to anyone who still thought Great Britain might yield, the long recital of 'injuries and indignities which have been heaped upon our country' since 1803, would surely show that Britain was determinedly hostile, that nothing short of war could shake her."[35] The full significance of Brown's observation is now more readily apparent, for it has been shown that the theme of British diabolism was the key in June 1812 in justifying a final call to arms. Furthermore, its emergence as a basic strategy for drawing upon the nation's vocabulary of acceptable motives was the product not only of the war Congress, but also of Republicans who between 1808 and 1811 gradually talked themselves into a test of British perseverance which could serve as the measure of Britain's unmitigated hostility toward American independence.

CHAPTER NINE

Beyond the Model to Symbolic Action

Our purpose has been to suggest a procedure for analyzing congressional behavior that explains how war was declared in 1812. Prior research has been guided primarily by a search for *causes* as antecedents of the war, a narrative scheme that reduces the complexities of decision making to an overly simplistic reconstruction of human motivation and conduct. Our procedure transforms this static view of the war's origins into a dynamic consideration of movement toward the concrete event of declaring war. We view three components of congressional behavior—partisanship, leadership, and rhetoric—as constituent parts of the decision-making process, not as causal agents.

In 1812, identification with party was requisite to establishing a pattern of cohesive group behavior among enough of the Republican members of the Congress to sustain the movement toward war. Whereas sectional, ideological, and other identifications divided rather than united the Congress, partisanship became the vehicle for organizing a majority representative of the nation as a whole. During the war session, in particular, southern and southeastern Republicans conquered sectional loyalties, which in previous years had sunk the embargo as a solution to the nation's foreign policy problems, by subsuming within the party's overall war position the pronavy legislation sponsored by northern Republicans. While not all Republicans were willing to include the navy in their war plans, the War Hawks demonstrated to their colleagues the strength of party cohesion on a national level. They showed how Republicans could act as a group in spite of strong conflicts among sectional interests.

To say, therefore, that the War of 1812 was a *Republican* war is to state only a half-truth. Republicans expected the war to unite rather than to divide the country. Further, they believed Americans would understand the war as a defense of national interests necessitated by the unmitigated hostility of Great Britain toward American independence. A group orientation based on sheer partisanship would have faltered short of war, as it did in 1798 and again in 1808. The voting of majority-party Federalists during John Adams's administration was a function of partisanship more than any other single factor, but the result was a divided, rather than integrated, stance on the question of war because Federalists failed to universalize the French threat to the nation. Similarly, Republicans in 1808 had the numbers to carry a prowar vote if they had been able as well to articulate a sufficiently compelling call to arms. Without such a call, sectional interests and divisions in the legislative party destroyed any effort to lead the nation into battle. Party unity had to be supplemented by a close identification with broad national concerns in order to maintain group cohesion around a policy of war.

It would be misleading, however, to portray the war solely as the product of partisanship reinforced by a close association of the party with the urgent national interests articulated by party rhetors. Without the additional factor of group-oriented leadership, the establishment of party unity in support of war legislation was impossible. Adams's failure to construct a group orientation among factionalized Federalists is a case in point. Believing that war would have further split his party as well as the nation, Adams increasingly withdrew during the war crisis with France. By way of contrast, Jefferson's conduct following the *Chesapeake* incident proved the importance of leadership by its very absence. He assumed that Republicans would automatically act together, just as they had since the Adams Congresses, and expected that party unity would continue no matter what the situation. His failure to maintain relationships between the executive and the Congress contributed to confusion within the ranks over the most appropriate course of action to be taken. Only Madison used the vehicle of partisanship, in consultation with key members of the House leadership, to build the consensus necessary for a declaration of war. Significantly, both Adams and Jefferson appreciated what Madison *did* in facilitating the group's movement toward the accomplishment of a goal with maximum advantage to its members.

In the end, war was the product of a group action made possible by the interaction of key factors. Partisanship was the basic behavioral pattern upon which leaders could build. Group-oriented leadership enabled the majority party to coordinate its efforts toward enactment of specific war legislation. Republican party rhetoric, as it evolved into a publicly defensible justification for war, transformed partisanship from a predictable behavior into a dynamic agent of the prowar program. Finally, with the party voting and speaking as a group, executive and legislative leaders effectively piloted the group toward a resolution of its foreign affairs problems.

It is our hope that this model of congressional behavior will be useful to scholars working in other periods or with other groups, but it should not be superimposed onto every war crisis. The three components of decision making in the war crises of early America were organically related in such a manner that a coordinated effort emerged toward the accomplishment of a specific goal, but the characteristics of that relationship will never recur exactly as they did then. Political decision making is a complex process involving choices that can never be perfectly modeled either by isolating the components of a process (as we have tried to do) or by describing the forces (ideological, economic, social, or whatever) that scholars presume to determine behavior. People do not respond mechanistically to crisis situations. Decisions to declare war are holistic responses to the demands of particular situations as defined by individuals acting in groups.

In 1812, the definition of the nation's situation that informed national leaders, more than any other, was a defense of republicanism. In chapter 1, we went beyond the republican synthesis in order to capture the dynamics of the process of declaring war. It is now necessary to go beyond the model and to specify how our study might help to illumine future studies of republicanism in the early republic and to show how for lawmakers in 1812 republicanism became symbolic action.

Republicanism, as Robert E. Shalhope recently noted, has been studied far more for the Revolutionary period than for the early republic. Assumptions to this point that politicians in the two periods understood the term in the same way downplay the possibility that the problems of the 1770s were different in important ways from those of the early nineteenth century. Undoubtedly, the founding fathers whose lifetimes spanned both periods saw themselves as continuing the struggles of the Revolution following the adoption of the Constitution, but as Bernard Bailyn reminds us, the 1780s and 1790s "cannot be understood in essentially ideological terms" but rather must be considered as a "product of a complicated interplay between the maturing of Revolutionary ideas and ideals and the involvements of everyday life—in politics, in business, and in the whole range of social activities." Our investigation of the Congress for the war crises of early America suggests that republican ideology provided decision makers only with what Shalhope terms "a framework for discussion."[1]

More precisely, republican ideology reinforced, but did not cause, the strong sense of group identity which enabled Republicans to declare war in 1812. A republican synthesis—reducing the complexities of partisanship, leadership, and rhetoric to manifestations of republican ideology—can never specify how language and ideas functioned in the early war crises. According to republican synthesists, maintaining the governing party's status became synonymous with preserving the nation's republican experiment, thereby requiring a declaration of war as proof that foreign challenges to America's honor and rights could be redressed by a government of the people. What can never be established by taking an exclusively ideological approach, however, is the manner in which Republicans brought ideology to bear on the particular circumstances of 1812. Why was it not an equally potent force during the crisis of 1807–08, following Britain's attack on the *Chesapeake*? Why were British abuses of national honor and maritime rights less critical to preserving republicanism in 1808? Why, for that matter, did Federalists fail to declare war in 1798 as a protection of the republican experiment against threats of Jacobinic subversion? These questions point toward the need to understand how the forces of ideology were eventually unleashed in the complex process that led to war.

The republican synthesis, in fact, actually dissolves at the point of explaining how the "defense of republicanism" theme guided the majority party's actions. At the behavioral level, there is an important distinction between Risjord's and Perkins's separate analyses of the role played by appeals to national honor. While Risjord explains that such appeals were sincere and eventually persuasive, Perkins understands them as mere rationalizations that offered the appearance of logical consistency where actually irrationality had prevailed. Even the association between Brown's "imperiled republic" and the national honor thesis is tenuous, for each points to a substantially different motive. While honor represented a call to defend national rights in order to avoid national disgrace, the imperiled republic represented a concern over power and survival, both by the governing party and for an untested form of popular government. In short, there has been little actual agreement over how Republicans arrived at their decision to defend the nation. Were they guided by considerations of power, motivated to avoid disgrace, or trapped by indecision and miscalculation into an irrational commitment? The answer is forthcoming only when we rephrase the question to emphasize the decision-making process over the static motives of decision makers and, from that perspective, identify how the verbal behavior of Republicans led to an opportunity to synthesize their otherwise disparate goals.

In particular, the emphasis on national honor has masked an important shift in the majority party's rhetoric, a shift that started at the time of the embargo and was completed by the beginning of the war session. It is true that national honor was among the most important themes of Republican spokesmen when the embargo was laid in 1807, that appeals were frequently made to vindicate America's rights as an independent power and to avoid the shame and humiliation that no proud nation should endure; but even then honor was beginning to be associated with a concern over the actual safety of the young republic. The denial of America's commercial rights, some suggested, represented more than just a loss of markets or a blow to national pride. It signaled a potential threat to sovereignty itself, the possibility of a British intention to undermine the independence of the American republic. Although the perception of such a threat was not yet compelling, and the prevailing image still allowed for influencing Great Britain's hostile intentions through the medium of economic coercion, the seed of suspicion had sprouted. If the British did not respond favorably to firm pressure from the embargo, Republicans reasoned, there could no longer be any doubt about the extent or intensity of their hostility toward America's independence. If nothing else, the language of Republican rhetors was suggestive of this ultimate threat. Images of the British were regularly rooted in metaphors of force which invited the direst expectations of attempted conquest. Yet until some firm stand was taken and maintained by the United States, there was not an adequate means of determining whether the image of a rational adversary responsive to economic pressures or the vision of an irrational enemy bent on dominance at any price would eventually prove to be the more accurate characterization of Great Britain. Honor was at stake, undoubtedly, but attention was already shifting toward the greater issue of sovereignty, i.e., the imperiled republic, as the nascent theme of British diabolism took root in Republican metaphors of force.

By 1812, Republican rhetors had articulated a justification for war based upon a full-fledged doctrine of British diabolism. America, they argued, was imperiled by the evil designs of a covetous enemy bent upon recolonizing its chief commercial rival in order to regain a lost monopoly over world trade. No longer could there be a significant doubt over the real intentions behind Britain's continued harassment of its former colonies. Each affront to the nation's honor, each attack on its interests, was now interpreted as a sure sign of the enemy's fixed and determined hostility toward America's independence. No incentive, economic pressure, or any other device short of war could induce the British to recede from their brutal scheme. Republican metaphors of force had been transformed into images of reality which portrayed the enemy as trampling on America's rights and wresting independence from its citizens in order to sate a bestial appetite for control of world commerce.

Such an appeal to diabolism spoke to the interests of the whole nation while it also reinforced latent concerns over the viability of republican government. If affronts to national honor and rights were actually symptoms of hostile intentions by the former mother country, then continued submission would lead not only to disgrace but also to destruction of the republican experiment. The party in power had to prove by repulsing the perceived threat that republicanism was neither a frail nor an impermanent form of government. Thus, the rhetoric of diabolism, as it led Republicans to construct an image of Britain's evil intentions, became a key to activating the full force of political ideology in 1812. The republic was in peril because Great Britain was perceived as intent upon its destruction, not because honor alone was at stake.

How was it that the image of British diabolism had congealed in 1812 when it was no more than emergent by the end of 1807? That is, how did this metamorphosis from suspicion to certitude come about? The answer, it seems, is found most directly in the rhetorical adaptations of Republicans between 1807 and 1812. Although partisanship and leadership remained as crucial components of the decision-making process, it was through the instrumentality of language that Republicans finally articulated the meaning of their situation so that all three components could become mutually reinforcing.

The most important development in the transition period of 1808–11 came with the passage of Macon's Bill #2 in May of 1810. Prior to that time, the test of Britain's true intentions depended upon the nation's ability to sustain a successful campaign of economic coercion. If the English could be made to feel the impact of restricted trade, it was reasoned, they would soon relinquish their attacks on American rights in order to preserve the best part of a mutually beneficial system of commerce. If, however, they did not recede in the face of an embargo, that would be seen as proof that the diabolical purpose of their aggression could be defeated only by a resort to arms. The obvious flaw in this test of British intentions was that it depended upon the nation's willingness to make major sacrifices without benefit of a compelling reason for all the parties involved. Consequently, embargo yielded to progressively weaker forms of resistance until Macon's Bill #2 all but ended the experiment in economic coercion. With the passage of the bill, Republicans turned to a passive test of British motives to replace the unrealistically demanding scheme of active resistance it had maintained since the end of 1807. The new test implicit in Macon's law could be implemented without undue reliance on American resolve. As the new symbol of American resistance, it required only the cooperation of an opportunistic Napoleon to measure the extent to which Britain would persist in its aggressions against commerce once the French Decrees had been "revoked." Republicans were then able to denounce the continuation of the Orders in Council as a final proof of Britain's intransigence and evil desire to recolonize America. It remained only for the members of the war Congress to dramatize the theme of recolonization as their publicly defensible justification for war.

Among the most important rhetorical adaptations of Republicans during this transition period, therefore, were those that facilitated the characterization of Macon's law, both before and after its enactment, as a symbol of American resistance and a test of British persistence. The hypothesis of evil intentions had already taken its form from the pervasion of metaphors of force, and the frequently cited history of British harassments was seen as consistent with that hypothesis. Attention had been focused on the very real possibility that Great Britain would stop at nothing to attain its coveted objective. As Congressman John Taylor pointed out, however, the nonintercourse law had made a mockery of the policy of economic resistance which his party had relied upon to test the hypothesis of evil intentions. The "honorable defense" had melted into thin air, leaving the nation without the final proof it needed of a British crusade against republicanism. Rather than continue the exercise in futility, he argued, the time had arrived for Congress to adopt a new strategy, one that placed the burden on the enemy to prove its good will.

Thus the logic of Macon's Bill #2 required that Britain show its ultimate respect for American rights and sovereignty by rescinding the Orders in Council so as to earn American support in the struggle against Napoleon's Decrees, or prove its inveterate hostility by holding fast to the Orders after the excuse of the Decrees had been removed. In either case, the initiative was with Britain, not the United States. When Napoleon made his qualified offer to withdraw the Decrees, Republican rhetors did everything possible to remove all doubts over the authenticity of his actions and then seized upon the opportunity to decry British recalcitrance. Republicans finally had found a way to affirm the most threatening expectations consistent with their image of British diabolism and thereby validate the hypothesis of evil intentions. Metaphors of force were no longer just figures of speech. They had been literalized by verifying their power to predict the course of Britain's campaign against American independence.

The significance of Republican rhetoric is more readily understood when compared with the failure of Federalists to justify war in 1798. Whereas Federalists had defined their crisis with France narrowly as an attack on commercial interests, Republicans universalized the threat by associating similar attacks on American commerce with affronts to national honor and rights and by interpreting such affronts as sure signs of a fixed and determined hostility toward the sovereignty of the United States. Federalist images of the crisis were further restricted by a language of seduction which minimized the threat of a French invasion, unlike Republican metaphors of force which emphasized the enemy's essential dependence upon power to achieve its ends. All that the logic of seduction demanded was that the nation remain alert and prepared. That alone was enough to discourage an adversary that relied primarily on deception to obtain its objectives. The worst expectations of Republican decision makers, for which confirmations were eventually found, were never so central to the language of Federalist decision makers. The crisis with France in 1798, therefore, was not a threat to the survival of the republic or republicanism. A rhetoric of diabolism had not evolved to release the force of political ideology as a unifying motive for war.

Those few Republicans who, along with the Federalists in Congress, resisted the declaration of war in 1812 never adopted the perspective taken by the majority of their party. In fact, as Randolph testified, they spoke a different language from those who had come to believe in the necessity of war with Great Britain. Foreign culprits and conspirators were a figment of imagination or, even worse, an excuse to commit aggression. Rather than preserving the republic, prowar Republicans were, from Randolph's point of view, destroying its most important principles. Pro- and antiwar Republicans, that is, spoke past one another, each side believing that it best served the vital interests of republicanism.

As is by now apparent, the dynamics of the decision-making process were far too complex for the ideology of republicanism to be considered *the explanation* of the war. Its application to the circumstances of 1812 was a product of interpretation unique to those in the group that voted for war. Others outside of the group and those who held power earlier did not share the same interpretation. Thus, for them, the ideology was either irrelevant to the events at hand or antithetical to a call to arms. We must, therefore, avoid the temptation to extend the insights of the republican synthesists beyond the limits of their usefulness. As Kenneth Burke has pointed out:

> The business of interpretation is accomplished by the two processes of over-simplification and analogical extension. We over-simplify a given event when we characterize it from the standpoint of a given interest— and we attempt to invent a similar characterization for other events by analogy. The great difficulty with the method in the judging of historical events is that it requires the rectification of false analogies through trial

and error, whereas the vast bungling complexes of history do not recur. For this reason, those who attempt to interpret history by ambitiously driven analogical extensions lay much emphasis upon the factors of history that can be called recurrent. But one can note the recurrent only by *abstracting* certain qualities from the given historical complexities. One must have special informing interests of his own.[2]

Burke's point is particularly valid for the War of 1812. Rather than projecting the concept of a republican synthesis onto the complex and diverse events of the early national period, research needs to be as flexible as the interpretations of those who participated in the events themselves. If politicians in the early republic found common ground in "republicanism," we must seek to understand how it became associated with their unique needs and individual interests. The majority in Congress finally constructed a perspective of republicanism, based on a rhetoric of diabolism, that seemed to justify the defense of the nation. They believed that their reasons were sound and publicly defensible, that the people would respond favorably to the call to arms. But that does not mean that others besides Republicans in Congress necessarily identified with republicanism and the war in the same fashion.

Despite the intensity of the group orientation of Republican congressmen, it is impossible to say to what degree Republican war justification reached the nation as a whole. It has long been popular to refer to the War of 1812 as the "Second War for American Independence," but historians should be cautious about projecting Republican congressional attitudes onto groups outside the capital. Traditional views that the first American party system was the national result of congressional infighting over Hamilton's financial plans and the wars of the French Revolution have been vigorously challenged in recent years by students of state politics who argue the reverse case. In Kentucky, for example, the same family-oriented political groups that existed in 1785 were present in 1792 at the time of statehood and formed the nucleus of the Federalist and Republican parties after 1793. Similarly, Jackson Turner Main has argued that "localist and cosmopolitan cultural outlooks" in most of the colonial assemblies are directly linked with Anti-Federalists and Federalists in the 1780s and with Republicans and Federalists in the 1790s. During the party-building of the 1790s "the national parties adapted to and modified . . . state blocs" rather than the reverse.

Until additional local studies systematically probe how partisan allegiances were formed, shifted, or were maintained from the late 1790s through the War of 1812, scholars would do well to follow Ronald P. Formisano's admonition that the peaks of partisanship in the Congress should not obscure the valleys of localism and factionalism in the nation at large.[3]

Finally, and at a higher level of abstraction, just as the declaration of war in 1812 can be understood as a product of group behavior, requiring the interaction of rhetoric with leadership and partisanship to embark upon a defense of republicanism, the establishment of a group orientation toward the war can itself be understood as an exercise in symbolic action. In Shalhope's terms, there is a "dramatic encounter between the internal world of images and meaning and the external one of circumstances and experience" which takes the form of symbolic action and leads to strategic responses in selectively perceived situations. Following Kenneth Burke's lead, Shalhope argues that the dynamic relationship of symbols and mind to environment dissolves "the familiar idealist-materialist dichotomy between thought and action."[4] Mind and environment encounter one another through the medium of verbal and nonverbal languages, or symbol systems, as Burke would say.[5] Meaning is constructed out of objective reality, that is, by treating aspects of social behavior and material conditions as symbols that stand for, represent, indicate, or participate in something else. In the case of 1812, each of the three components of congressional behavior was part of this larger process. Together they were more than just a complex of objective behaviors in the realm of motion because they were also interpreted by those who participated in the act of decision making. They became a shared language, or system of symbols, which defined a situation for the group that was conducive to the declaration of war. Each aspect of behavior was a mode of symbolic action in the ongoing process of interpreting reality that led finally to the point of deciding for war.

The direction in which to proceed, then, is toward an explicit understanding of how behavior functioned as symbolic action, i.e., how it worked as an instrument of adjusting to a given situation. Rather than searching for causes of behavior, and thereby assuming that they actually constrained decisions to the point of eliminating all significant opportunities for choosing one course of action over others, it is more revealing to examine the patterns of conduct that took on meaning for the actors themselves. As Shalhope concludes, "republicanism alone does not constitute a sufficient cause or motive to explain action."[6] Nor does any other cause or set of causes. Instead, we can explain how the salience of republicanism became apparent to the particular group in its particular circumstances. Regarding the declaration of war, that means searching out the message constructed in Congress from the words, votes, and interactions of decision makers, while recognizing that the message itself fluctuated over time. The meaning of a given vote or speech changed as its overall context was altered by other symbolic acts, until the give-and-take culminated in a coordinated interpretation of reality. More specifically, the "language" of partisan voting and group-oriented leadership reinforced the rhetoric of diabolism, eventually to transform perceived reality into an agreed-upon threat to republicanism.

Viewed as the actions of symbol users attempting to make sense of a complex and changing situation, the patterns of congressional behavior described in this study appear as a web of meaning fortified at key points and reworked where necessary to compensate for its surroundings. Each new strand was adjusted to prevailing circumstances until the web was well-enough formed to ensnare its own makers.

One of the best illustrations of behavior as symbolic action was the point at which Republicans from the South began to vote in increasing numbers for legislation designed to strengthen the navy. The general upswing in party voting, in fact, marked a significant degree of party unity on even the most divisive issues. Prior to that time, fragmentation of Republicans over the issue of the navy had contributed to repeal of the embargo and adoption of nonintercourse for lack of better alternatives upon which party members from various regions of the country could agree. When Republicans no longer let their differences over the navy derail partisan voting on other foreign policy issues, they created a symbol of unity which meant that support for war legislation could be counted upon by the leadership in Congress. At the same time, Madison's willingness to work closely with congressional leaders signaled his administration's support for war and contributed further to the growing understanding among Republicans. The message of a Republican consensus was articulated, that is, through the language of voting and leadership behavior. Consensus at that level could only make agreement on the rhetoric of diabolism so much the easier to achieve. As a cohesive majority of Republicans talked among themselves about the evidence of Britain's evil intentions, ignoring the arguments of Federalists and minority members of their own party, they diminished any exposure to criticism from others that would have undermined confidence in the justification for war. The message of cohesion increased confidence in the rationale for defending the republic from its enemies.

The inherent flexibility of symbolic action was also evident in the Republicans' movement toward war. Theirs was no simple, linear progression from peace to war. Instead, they adapted continuously to the fluid situation as it evolved largely from their own actions. Their behavior, in other words, was self-reflexive. It was both an outcome of symbolic action and a medium for interpreting its own creations. What was at one moment an act of interpretation became at the next moment a datum for interpretation. The meaning constructed in an earlier circumstance was subject later to reconstruction. As a result, the war movement amounted essentially to an opportunistic process of defining and redefining a constantly emerging situation until a point was reached where it seemed most appropriate to call the nation to arms.

Republican verbal behavior in particular displayed a dexterity which enabled party members to reassess the meaning of ongoing events as opportunities arose. Napoleon's ambiguous response to Macon's bill, for instance, was rhetorically transformed into an absolute extinction of the French Decrees, and Britain's unwillingness to revoke the Orders in Council became complete proof of an intent to destroy the United States. Such extreme conclusions were made easier by assigning a greater clarity of purpose to Macon's bill after the fact than was apparent to the majority of legislators when it was originally passed. In retrospect, the law seemed a very deliberate and precise experiment to test the true extent of Britain's hostility. Prior to Napoleon's gesture, however, it was understood by many as amounting to a retreat from the defense of America's commercial rights and by others as having the potential for selecting one foe over the other. The grounds upon which the law was at first proposed, that is, contained the kernel of an idea which Republican rhetors later developed into a stronger hybrid for condemning British diabolism.

Instances of symbolic dexterity such as these were central, not peripheral, to the decision to declare war. They were instrumental in constructing an interpretation of reality which legitimized the defense of republicanism. The only other way that Republicans could have made sense out of the world they encountered was to acknowledge the essentially irrational nature of the war's origins and conclusion: that the "causes" of the war were better located in periods prior to 1812 than in that year; that Madison was an unlikely war president compared to Washington, Jefferson, or even Adams; that the war, begun in great optimism by the majority party, was at best inglorious and nearly disastrous; and that during and following the war, the majority party adopted the bulk of the Federalist program of the 1790s. The eventual outcome of their deliberations was neither pre-determined nor accidental, neither rational nor irrational. It was instead a strategic adaptation, a symbolic encompassment of competing interests, ideas, and perceptions—an attempt to make whole the broken pieces of reality.

Notes

Chapter One

1. Warren H. Goodman, "The Origins of the War of 1812: A Survey of Changing Interpretations," *Mississippi Valley Historical Review* 28 (1941–42): 171–86. For an update of Goodman's article, see Clifford L. Egan, "The Origins of the War of 1812: Three Decades of Historical Writing," *Military Affairs* 38 (1974): 72–75. For a review of the political origins of the war that stresses the partisan environment within which the declaration occurred, see Ronald L. Hatzenbuehler, "Party Unity and the Decision for War in the House of Representatives, 1812," *William and Mary Quarterly*, 3d ser., 29 (1972): 367–90.

2. John R. Howe, *From the Revolution Through the Age of Jackson: Innocence and Empire in the Young Republic* (Englewood Cliffs, N.J.: Prentice-Hall, 1973), p. 90. The standard account of the war's origins that emphasizes that the war was a response to European problems is Reginald Horsman, *The Causes of the War of 1812* (Philadelphia: Univ. of Pennsylvnia Press, 1962).

3. Robert E. Shalhope, "Toward a Republican Synthesis: The Emergence of an Understanding of Republicanism in American Historiography," *William and Mary Quarterly*, 3d ser., 29 (1972): 49–80; "Republicanism and Early American Historiography," *William and Mary Quarterly*, 3d ser., 39 (1982): 334–56.

4. Richard Hofstadter, *The Idea of a Party System: The Rise of Legitimate Opposition in the United States, 1780–1840* (Berkeley and Los Angeles: Univ. of California Press, 1969), p. 181.

5. J. C. A. Stagg, "James Madison and the 'Malcontents': The Political Origins of the War of 1812," *William and Mary Quarterly*, 3d ser., 33 (1976): 557.

6. Norman K. Risjord, "1812: Conservatives, War Hawks, and the Nation's Honor," *William and Mary Quarterly*, 3d ser., 18 (1961): 200, 204; Risjord, *The Old Republicans: Southern Conservatism in the Age of Jefferson* (New York: Columbia Univ. Press, 1965), pp. 96–145; Margaret Kinard Latimer, "South Carolina—A Protagonist of the War of 1812," *American Historical Review* 61 (1956): 914–29. Latimer, in turn, was heavily influenced by George Rogers Taylor. See Taylor, "Prices in the Mississippi Valley Preceding the War of 1812," *Journal of Economic and Business History* 3 (1930): 148–63, and "Agrarian Discontent in the Mississippi Valley Preceding the War of 1812," *Journal of Political Economy* 39 (1931): 471–505.

7. Bradford Perkins, *Prologue to War: England and the United States, 1805–1812* (Berkeley and Los Angeles: Univ. of California Press, 1961), p. vii. See esp. pp. 346–47, 373–77, 425.

8. Roger H. Brown, *The Republic in Peril: 1812* (New York: Columbia Univ. Press, 1964).

9. Ibid., p. vii.

10. Gordon H. Wood, *The Creation of the American Republic, 1776–1787* (Chapel Hill: Univ. of North Carolina Press, 1969).

11. John R. Howe, "Republican Thought and the Political Violence of the 1790s," *American Quarterly* 19 (1967): 147–65; Richard Buel, Jr., *Securing the Revolution: Ideology in American Politics, 1789–1815* (Ithaca: Cornell Univ. Press, 1972), pp. 51–52.

12. Lance G. Banning, *The Jeffersonian Persuasion: Evolution of a Party Ideology* (Ithaca: Cornell Univ. Press, 1978); J. G. A. Pocock, *The Machiavellian Moment: Florentine Political Thought and the Atlantic Republican Tradition* (Princeton: Princeton Univ. Press, 1975), p. 529; Drew R. McCoy, *The Elusive Republic: Political Economy in Jeffersonian America* (Chapel Hill: Univ. of North Carolina Press, 1980), p. 10; Banning, "The Moderate as Revolutionary: An Introduction to Madison's Life," *The Quarterly Journal of the Library of Congress* 37 (1980): 162–75 (Banning's forthcoming biography of Madison is announced on p. 162). See also Banning's review of *The Elusive Republic* in *Journal of American History* 68 (1981): 123–24.

13. Risjord, "Conservatives, War Hawks, and the Nation's Honor," pp. 200, 204. Brown, *Republic in Peril*, pp. 86–87.

14. Perkins, *Prologue to War*, pp. 433–37; Bernard Bailyn, et al., *The Great Republic: A History of the American People*, 2 vols. (Lexington, Ma.: D. C. Heath, 1979), I: 388.

15. Shalhope, "Toward a Republican Synthesis," p. 73.

16. David H. Fischer, *The Revolution of American Conservatism: The Federalist Party in the Era of Jeffersonian Democracy* (New York: Harper & Row, 1965); Linda K. Kerber, *Federalists in Dissent: Imagery and Ideology in Jeffersonian America* (Ithaca: Cornell Univ. Press, 1970); Gerald Stourzh, *Alexander Hamilton and the Idea of Republican Government* (Stanford: Stanford Univ. Press, 1970); and James M. Banner, Jr., *To the Hartford Convention: The Federalists and the Origins of Party Politics in Massachusetts, 1789–1815* (New York: Alfred A. Knopf, 1970).

17. Banner, *To the Hartford Convention*, pp. 40, 42–43, 51.

18. Risjord, *The Old Republicans*; Noble E. Cunningham, Jr., "Who Were the Quids?" *Mississippi Valley Historical Review* 50 (1963): 252–63; Robert Dawidoff, *The Education of John Randolph* (New York: W. W. Norton, 1979), pp. 30, 197.

19. Shalhope, "Toward a Republican Synthesis," p. 72; Shalhope's review of Leslie Wharton, *Party and the Public Good*, in *Journal of American History* 68 (1981): 370.

20. Leland R. Johnson, "The Suspense Was Hell: The Senate Vote for War in 1812," *Indiana Magazine of History* 65 (1969): 247–67.

21. Robert P. Swierenga, "Computers and American History: The Impact of the 'New' Generation," *Journal of American History* 60 (1974): 1053.

22. Rudolph M. Bell, "Mr. Madison's War and Long-Term Congressional Voting Behavior," *William and Mary Quarterly*, 3d ser., 36 (1979): 373–95.

23. Ronald L. Hatzenbuehler and Robert L. Ivie, "Justifying the War of 1812: Toward a Model of Congressional Behavior in Early War Crises," *Social Science History* 4 (1980): 455–57.

24. Ronald L. Hatzenbuehler, "Foreign Policy Voting in the U. S. Congress, 1808–1812" (Ph.D. diss., Kent State University, 1972).

25. Stagg, "Madison and the 'Malcontents';" Ronald L. Hatzenbuehler, "The War Hawks and the Question of Leadership in 1812," *Pacific Historical Review* 45 (1976): 1–22; Harry W. Fritz, "The War Hawks of 1812: Party Leadership in the Twelfth Congress," *Capitol Studies* 5 (1977): 25–42.

Chapter Two

1. Richard H. Kohn, *Eagle and Sword: The Federalists and the Creation of the Military Establishment, 1783–1802* (New York: Free Press, 1975).

2. J. C. A. Stagg, "James Madison and the Coercion of Great Britain: Canada, the West Indies, and the War of 1812," *William and Mary Quarterly*, 3d ser., 38 (1981): 3–34.

3. Thomas A. Bailey, *Presidential Greatness: The Image and the Man from George Washington to the Present* (New York: Appleton-Century, 1966), pp. 24–25, 33–34.

4. Fred E. Fiedler and Martin M. Chemers, *Leadership and Effective Management* (Glenview, Ill.: Scott, Foresman, 1974), p. 63 ff. See also for the importance of group pressures on the leader: E. P. Hollander, *Leaders, Groups, and Influence* (New York: Oxford Univ. Press, 1964); and Fred E. Fiedler, "Validation and Extension of the Contingency Model of Leadership Effectiveness," *Psychological Bulletin* 75 (1971): 128–48. Similarly, Richard Neustadt's "role analysis" emphasizes the group relationships between leader and followers. As applied to Thomas Jefferson's presidency, see Robert M. Johnstone, Jr., *Jefferson and the Presidency: Leadership in the Young Republic* (Ithaca: Cornell Univ. Press, 1978) and chapter 6 in this book.

5. Paul F. Secord and Carl W. Backman, *Social Psychology* (New York: McGraw-Hill, 1964), p. 354. See also Robert A. Baron, et al., *Social Psychology: Understanding Human Interaction* (Boston: Allyn & Bacon, 1974), p. 455.

6. Reginald Horsman, "Who Were the War Hawks?" *Indiana Magazine of History* 60 (1964): 132. See also Bernard Mayo, *Henry Clay: Spokesman of the New West* (1937; rpt. ed., Hamden, Ct.: Archon Books, 1966), pp. 385–426; John S. Pancake, "The 'Invisibles': A Chapter in the Opposition to President Madison," *Journal of Southern History* 12 (1955): 17–37; and Margaret K. Latimer, "South Carolina—A Protagonist of the War of 1812," *American Historical Review* 41 (1956): 914–29.

7. Norman K. Risjord, "1812: Conservatives, War Hawks, and the Nation's Honor," *William and Mary Quarterly*, 3d ser., 18 (1961): 196–210; Bradford Perkins, *Prologue to War: England and the United States, 1805–1812* (Berkeley and Los Angeles: Univ. of California Press, 1961), pp. 346–50; 377–417; Roger H. Brown, *The Republic in Peril, 1812* (New York: Columbia Univ. Press, 1964); and Brown, "The War Hawks of 1812: An Historical Myth," *Indiana Magazine of History* 60 (1964): 138–51. See also Clifford L. Egan, "The Origins of the War of 1812: Three Decades of Historical Writing," *Military Affairs* 38 (1974): 72–75.

8. Harry W. Fritz, "The War Hawks of 1812: Party Leadership in the Twelfth Congress," *Capitol Studies* 5(1977): 25–42.

9. R. L. Hatzenbuehler, "The War Hawks and the Question of Congressional Leadership in 1812," *Pacific Historical Review* 45 (1976): 1–22; Horsman, "War Hawks," pp. 125, 129, 130.

10. Allan G. Bogue, "Some Dimensions of Power in the Thirty-Seventh Senate," in William O. Aydelotte, et al., eds., *The Dimensions of Quantitative Research in History* (Princeton: Princeton Univ. Press, 1972), pp. 285–318.

11. This table is taken from the ICPSR data sheets and is misleading in some instances. The bulk of Bacon's bills resulted from a single Ways and Means Committee report on taxes, whereas Porter's originated throughout the session. Likewise, Langdon Cheves's perfect record of success does not reflect the fact that he was unable to carry that part of his naval report which asked the Congress to build new frigates.

12. No minutes exist for the Ways and Means Committee comparable to those of the Foreign Relations Committee. When assessed in terms of the number of different bills authored in Congress, however, the Foreign Relations Committee emerges as the most important congressional committee of the session. The success rate of the committee, incidentally,

compares very favorably with modern congressional committees. See Lawrence C. Dodd, "Committee Integration in the Senate: A Comparative Analysis," *Journal of Politics* 34 (1972): 1135–71; and Alan Rosenthal, "Legislative Committee Systems: An Exploratory Analysis," *Western Political Quarterly* 26 (1973): 252–62.

13. *Annals of Congress*, 12th Cong., 1st sess.: 342–43.

14. Ibid.: 333, 342–43. The figure for freshman Republican legislators alone is 45 percent. Today, by contrast, about 75 percent of the majority-party, freshmen congressmen receive seats on committees. David W. Rohde and Kenneth A. Shepsle, "Democratic Committee Assignments in the House of Representatives: Strategic Aspects of a Social Choice Process," *American Political Science Review* 67 (1973): 889–905; and Charles S. Bullock III, "Freshman Committee Assignments and Re-election in the United States House of Representatives," *American Political Science Review* 66 (1972): 996–1007.

15. Mayo, *Henry Clay*, p. 410; Glyndon G. Van Deusen, *The Life of Henry Clay* (Boston: Little, Brown and Company, 1937), pp. 78–79; Perkins, *Prologue to War*, pp. 346–47; Ralph Ketcham, *James Madison: A Biography* (New York: Macmillan, 1971), pp. 508–29, 512; and Harry Ammon, *James Monroe: The Quest for the National Identity* (New York: McGraw-Hill, 1971), p. 301. Ammon incorrectly labels Federalist "Philip M. Key" [*sic*] a War Hawk.

16. William Lowndes to Elizabeth Lowndes, 2 or 3 November 1811, in Harriott H. R. Ravenel, *Life and Times of William Lowndes of South Carolina* (Boston: Houghton, Mifflin, 1901), p. 84. For the importance of the boardinghouses, see James S. Young, *The Washington Community* (New York: Harcourt, Brace & World, 1966) as modified by Allan G. Bogue and Mark Paul Marlaire, "Of Mess and Men: The Boardinghouse and Congressional Voting, 1821–1842," *American Journal of Political Science* 19 (1975): 207–30. Strikingly, two other members of the mess, South Carolinians William Lowndes and Langdon Cheves, were members of the Commerce and Manufactures and Ways and Means committees, respectively. *Annals of Congress*, 12th Cong., 1st sess.: 333. William Plumer to Henry Clay, 20 November 1811, in James F. Hopkins, ed., *The Papers of Henry Clay* 5 vols. (Lexington, Ky.: Univ. of Kentucky Press, 1959), I: 598. Harper kept Plumer well informed about House proceedings. See the William Plumer Letterbooks, Manuscript Division, Library of Congress, reprinted in Clifford L. Egan, "The Path to War in 1812 through the Eyes of a New Hampshire 'War Hawk,' " *Historical New Hampshire* 30 (1975): 147–77.

17. There is no clear explanation for multiple committee assignments. Seniority, youth, partisanship, friendship with Clay, prowar enthusiasm—all doubtlessly explain the assignments (see Table 2.3).

18. On February 27, 1812, Porter seconded a motion made by Republican James Fisk of Vermont to postpone the war taxes until after war had been declared. He said he would vote for war and taxes if proposed "without reserve . . . but he wished not to lay them by anticipation." *Annals of Congress*, 12th Cong., 1st sess.: 1109, 1594. Peter B. Porter to William Eustis, 19 and 20 April, 1812, Records of the Office of the Secretary of War, Letters Received (Microfilm 221, Roll 47), #P98 (1812), National Archives. We are indebted to Roger Brown for helping to locate these important letters which conclusively dispel the notion that Porter was a War Hawk. Brown, *Republic in Peril*, pp. 131–33; *Annals of Congress*, 12th Cong., 1st sess.: 1635.

19. Felix Grundy to Andrew Jackson, 28 November 1811, Andrew Jackson Papers, Manuscript Division, Library of Congress.

20. Ibid.; see also William Lowndes to Elizabeth Lowndes, 7 December 1811, in Ravenel, *William Lowndes*, p. 90. Minutes of the Committee of Foreign Relations, 6 February 1812, file A-2, Peter B. Porter Papers, Buffalo and Erie Historical Society.

21. Minutes of the Committee of Foreign Relations, 11 February 1812, ibid. Madison, in the same interview, said that "[i]f he were to express any wish on the subject," he would

Table 2.3
Republicans on More than One Committee:
Twelfth House, First Session

Four		Three		Two	
Morrow	Oh	Bibb	Ga	Blackledge	NC
		McKee	Ky	Brown	Pa
		Porter	NY	Butler	SC
		Seybert	Pa	Cheves	SC
				Desha	Ky
				Grundy	Te
				Little	Md
				Macon	NC
				McKim	Md
				Milnor	Pa
				Mitchill	NY
				Newton	Va
				Shaw	Vt
				Smilie	Pa
				Williams	SC
				Wright	Md

prefer that 10,000 to 12,000 of the 25,000 troops authorized by Congress be raised for one or two rather than five years. One might infer from this remark that the president was "hedging" on the war issue and that the Foreign Affairs Committee was far ahead of him. At the same meeting, however, Porter proposed (and only Harper agreed) that an additional force of 20,000 troops be raised for service at any time within two years, and the measure was soundly defeated. The committee, in other words, struck a middle course between the two alternatives.

22. In the letter of March 24, Porter told Monroe that the committee wanted "to ascertain the views of the Executive on the following points": 1) if the forces provided for were adequate; 2) when the committee might "calculate that the military preparations now going on, under the direction of the Executive, will be in a state to justify the commencement of open active hostilities against G. Britain"; and 3) whether it was "advisable that a declaration of War should be preceded by an Embargo." Peter B. Porter to James Monroe, 24 March 1812, file A-9, ibid. Also, see Henry Clay to James Monroe, 15 March 1812, in Hopkins, *Papers*, I: 637.

23. The minutes of the March 30 and 31 meetings are contained in the Samuel Smith Papers, Manuscript Division, Library of Congress. The meeting was probably a joint one between House and Senate committees dealing with foreign affairs. The minutes are in Samuel Smith's handwriting, and his editorial remarks are easily separated from the recorded questions and answers. At the beginning of the memo, Monroe's answers to committee members' questions are within quotation marks, but his answers later in the memo are not within quotation marks.

24. *Annals of Congress*, 12th Cong. 1st sess.: 1587.

25. Monroe's role is emphasized in Harry Ammon's recent biography of the secretary of state. Bradford Perkins concludes from his analysis of the committee reports that the Congress had to push Monroe and Madison continually to force the executive branch into action. Irving Brant, however, sees Madison leading Congress slowly toward war in order to unite the

country and to gain as many adherents for war as possible. Ralph Ketcham's biography of Madison blames the executive for the unprepared state of the nation in 1812 and suggests that Madison was hampered by "misjudgments, too-subtle policies, and republican predilections." Harold S. Schultz has recently concluded that Madison's constitutional beliefs caused the president to create suspicion about the progress of the administration's war policies. Ammon, *James Monroe*, p. 301; Perkins, *Prologue to War*, p. 349; Irving Brant, *James Madison: The President, 1809-1812* (Indianapolis: Bobbs-Merrill, 1956), esp. pp. 437-83; Ketcham, *James Madison*, pp. 531-33; Harold S. Schultz, *James Madison* (New York: Twayne, 1970), p. 155. See also the exchange of letters between D. R. Hickey and R. L. Hatzenbuehler, *Pacific Historical Review* 45 (1976): 642-45.

26. James Madison to William Pinkney, 1 January 1810 in Ketcham, *James Madison*, p. 498.

27. Nathaniel Macon claimed only to be "step father" to the bills, which he said were a "cabinet project." Nathaniel Macon to Joseph H. Nicholson, 21 April 1810, in William E. Dodd, ed., *John P. Branch Historical Papers of Randolph Macon College* 3 (1909): 61-62. In a letter of April 10, Macon declared that his second bill was really John Taylor's (ibid., pp. 60-61). Madison had long favored such a plan as Macon's Bill #2. Writing to John Armstrong early in 1808, Madison said, "The relation in which a recall of its retaliating decrees by either power, will place the United States to the other is obvious; and ought to be a motive to the measure proportioned to the desire which has been manifested by each, to produce collisions between the U. States and its adversary and which must be equally felt by each to avoid one with itself." James Madison to John Armstrong, 2 May 1808, in Gaillard Hunt, ed., *The Writings of James Madison* 9 vols. (New York: G. P. Putnam's Sons, 1908), VIII: 27.

28. "Memorandum as to Robert Smith," April 1811, Madison Papers, Library of Congress; Hunt, *Writings of James Madison*, VIII: 140-41.

29. Because of the consensus established by Macon's Bill #2, the critical point in Republican cohesion appears to have been passed during the third session of the Eleventh Congress. During the third session, Republican partisanship reached levels significantly higher (p < .01) than during either previous session or during the war session of the Twelfth Congress. In addition, both parties reached their zeniths of partisanship during the critical third session. Partisanship is defined as occurring when 90 percent of all legislators voted along party lines on an individual roll call. The figures within parentheses represent the number of roll calls in which one party attained unanimity.

Table 2.4
Partisan and Nonpartisan Foreign Policy Votes, 1808-1812

	Partisan		Nonpartisan	
	No.	Percent	No.	Percent
Tenth House, Second Session	21 (13)	21.9	75	78.1
Eleventh House, First Session	1 (0)	7.1	13	92.8
Eleventh House, Second Session	46 (16)	44.7	57	55.3
Eleventh House, Third Session	34 (2)	53.1	30	46.9
Twelfth House, First Session	32 (7)	28.3	81	71.7

30. Henry Clay to Caesar A. Rodney, 11 January 1811, Misc. Personal File, Caesar A. Rodney Papers, Library of Congress.

31. Herman Knickerbocker to Harmanus Bleecker, 7 January 1811, Harmanus Bleecker Papers, New York State Library. Abijah Bigelow to Hannah Bigelow, 21 January 1811, in American Antiquarian Society, *Proceedings*, n.s. 40 (1931), 315; Samuel Taggart to John Taylor, 4 February 1811, ibid., 38 (1923), 355.

32. "Memorandum as to Robert Smith," in Hunt, *Writings of James Madison*, VIII: 138–44.

33. In framing the tax package, Albert Gallatin worked as closely with the Ways and Means Committee as Monroe did with the Foreign Relations Committee. Gallatin, in fact, wrote Ezekiel Bacon's tax resolutions which the Massachusetts legislator introduced on February 17, 1812. Albert Gallatin to Ezekiel Bacon, 10 January 1812, in Adams, ed., *Writings of Albert Gallatin*, 3 vols. (Philadelphia: J. B. Lippincott, 1879), I: 501–17; *Annals of Congress*, 12th Cong., 1st sess.: 1106–7.

34. James Monroe to John Taylor, 13 June 1812, James Monroe Papers, Library of Congress.

35. Harry Ammon argues that the final war decision came in August 1811 during a meeting at Montpelier: "It seems likely that Monroe and Madison at this time reached an agreement to move toward war if Great Britain did not respond to American demands by the end of the year." Ammon, *James Monroe*, p. 299; see also Ketcham, *James Madison*, p. 508. Lawrence S. Kaplan explains the timing of the decision in terms of calculations based upon France's European war goals—especially the Russian invasion. Harold S. Schultz feels the election of 1812 spurred Madison's timing. Lawrence S. Kaplan, "France and Madison's Decision for War, 1812," *Mississippi Valley Historical Review* (1964): 652–71; Schultz, *James Madison*, pp. 155–56. For an analysis of the domestic pressures on Madison, see J. C. A. Stagg, "James Madison and the 'Malcontents:' The Political Origins of the War of 1812," *William and Mary Quarterly*, 3d ser., 33 (1976): 557–85.

36. Abbott Smith, "Mr. Madison's War: An Unsuccessful Experiment in the Conduct of National Policy," *Political Science Quarterly* 57 (1942): 229–46; Rudolph M. Bell, "Mr. Madison's War and Long-Term Congressional Voting Behavior," *William and Mary Quarterly*, 3d ser., 36 (1979): 373–95.

37. Hollander, *Leaders*, p. 225.

Chapter Three

1. *Annals of Congress*, 12th Cong., 1st sess., 11–15, 373–77. Bradford Perkins suggests the message would have been even stronger had Gallatin not persuaded the president to weaken his statements. *Prologue to War: England and the United States, 1805–1812* (Berkeley and Los Angeles: Univ. of California Press, 1961), pp. 296–97.

2. Scales available upon request.

3. *Annals of Congress*, 12th Cong., 1st sess.: 595–691; 602.

4. Ibid., 441–55, quote on 455; 511–16.

5. Ibid., 519, 679.

6. Ibid., 423–24.

7. Ibid., 1050–56; 1106–7. This report was prepared essentially by Albert Gallatin. Albert Gallatin to Ezekiel Bacon, Jan. 10, 1812. Henry Adams, ed., *The Writings of Albert Gallatin*, 3 vols. (Philadelphia: J. B. Lippincott, 1879), I: 501–17.

8. *Annals of Congress*, 12th Cong., 1st sess.: 1093–1105.

9. Ibid., 1114–15.

10. Benjamin Tallmadge to James McHenry, 29 February 1812. James McHenry Papers, 2d ser., vol. 7, Library of Congress. Emphasis in original.

11. *Annals of Congress*, 12th Cong., 1st sess.: 1117–19.

12. John A. Harper to William Plumer, 11 March 1812. William Plumer Papers, Library of Congress.

13. *Annals of Congress*, 12th Cong., 1st sess.: 553–56.

14. Ibid., 803–16; quote on p. 803.

15. Ibid., 1004.

16. For a discussion of the techniques of cluster-bloc analysis and the index of cohesion, see R. L. Hatzenbuehler, "Party Unity and the Decision for War in the House of Representatives, 1812," *William and Mary Quarterly*, 3d ser., 29 (1972), 553–64, with the modification that only: 1) unanimous roll calls, and 2) legislators who voted less than 50 percent of the time with their colleagues were excluded from the analysis. With regard to the calculations in Table 3.2, there is no "magic" level of cohesion that will best measure pair-wise voting in any situation. In the Adams Congresses, the average level of cohesion for each session was well above 70 (a cohesion index of 40, or a 70/30 percent split), but the Jefferson Congresses at times had trouble attaining this level. Republicans in the war session needed to attain that level in order to declare war (in fact, they surpassed it). In order to be defined as a member of a "bloc," therefore, a congressman had to: 1) vote with another member on at least 50 percent of the roll calls; 2) achieve a level of agreement of 70 percent of the other group members. In other words, the first step was to isolate the member of the group in the section who voted with the largest number of his colleagues. That number became the base figure. In order to be a member of that bloc, a legislator had to have voted 70 percent of the time with 70 percent of the base figure. A member of the "fringe" failed to meet the second criterion of voting with 70 percent of the base figure. The 100 cluster-blocs used in this study are available on request.

Chapter Four

1. C. Wright Mills, "Situated Actions and Vocabularies of Motive," *American Sociological Review* 5 (1940): 907–10.

2. Kenneth E. Boulding, "National Images and International Systems," *Journal of Conflict Resolution* 3 (1959): 121–22.

3. Ibid., p. 120. See also Ole R. Holsti, "The Belief System and National Images: A Case Study," *Journal of Conflict Resolution* 6 (1962): 244–52.

4. Robert E. Shalhope, "Toward a Republican Synthesis: The Emergence of an Understanding of Republicanism in American Historiography," *William and Mary Quarterly*, 3d ser., 29 (1972): 79–80. See also Gene Wise, "Political 'Reality' in Recent American Scholarship: Progressives versus Symbolists," *American Quarterly* 19 (1967): 303–28. The concept of symbolic action and its relevance to rhetoric has been developed primarily by Kenneth Burke in his several works, including *The Philosophy of Literary Form: Studies in Symbolic Action* (1941; rpt. New York: Vintage Books, 1957), *A Rhetoric of Motives* (1950; rpt. Berkeley and Los Angeles: Univ. of California Press, 1969), *Permanence and Change: An Anatomy of Purpose*, 2d ed. (1954; rpt. Indianapolis: Bobbs-Merrill, 1965), and "Dramatism," in *Communication Concepts and Perspectives*, ed. Lee Thayer (Washington, D.C.: Spartan Books, 1967), pp. 327–60. For a general discussion of the functions and effects of verbal behavior, see Doris A. Graber, *Verbal Behavior and Politics* (Urbana: Univ. of Illinois Press, 1976), ch. 3.

5. The recurrent themes (Table 4.1) were identified originally by reading through the debates in the Fifth, Tenth, and Twelfth Congresses and listing the issues and arguments that were addressed by majority party speakers in the House on war-related topics. A number of secondary works on the historical period were also consulted to determine whether any additional items should be added to the list. The combined list was then revised to eliminate obvious redundancies and to organize items into more general thematic units. This procedure is similar to "maximal theme analysis" as discussed by Thomas F. Carney, *Content Analysis: A Technique for Systematic Inference from Communications* (Winnipeg, Canada: Univ. of Manitoba Press, 1972), pp. 159–63.

6. The coding for the study was done by Ivie and checked independently by Hatzen-

buehler and Steven Miura, who was at the time a doctoral student in Speech at Washington State University. Given the detail of the coding system, it was most efficient to have the two react to the original coding by circling each code mark with which they disagreed. A sample of 396 lines (4 percent of the discourse coded and reported in chapters 4, 5, and 6) was checked, including one column from two different documents for each of the three Congresses (*Annals of Congress*, Wright: 468; and Calhoun: 477 from the Twelfth Congress; Johnson: 1152; and Fisk: 2111 from the first session of the Tenth Congress; and Allen: 1477; and Sitgreaves: 1902 from the second session of the Fifth Congress). Miura's overall agreement with the original coding was .98 (ranging from .94 to 1.00). Hatzenbuehler's average rate of agreement was .96 (ranging from .81 to 1.00). A judgmental sample of speakers and speeches was made in order to ensure the selection of the most topical texts, i.e., those that focused most directly on the issue of war. Speakers were selected on the basis of two criteria: (1) that they articulated their positions in rather extended statements before the Congress, and (2) that, as a group, they represented those who were strongly committed to voting by party based upon the scales of foreign policy votes in each Congress. Of an estimated 12,740 lines of war-related discourse in the Fifth Congress, second session, the five speakers who were sampled produced 10,098 lines or 80 percent of the discourse. We sampled 2,369 lines, amounting to 19 percent of the Federalist war discourse and 24 percent of the sampled speakers' war discourse. In the first session of the Tenth Congress, Republicans produced an estimated 11,880 lines of war discourse, 62 percent of which (7,326) came from the speakers sampled. Our sample of 3,593 lines amounted to 29 percent of Republican war discourse and 48 percent of the sampled speakers' war discourse. In the first session of the Twelfth Congress, majority party representatives produced an estimated 16,500 lines of war-related discourse. The speakers from whom samples were drawn produced 6,996 of these lines (42 percent). We sampled 3,524 lines, or 20 percent of Republican war discourse, and 48 percent of the lines produced by the sample of speakers. If this had been a random sample, we would have needed to sample about 665 lines from each Congress in order to estimate thematic densities as reported in Tables 4.2, 5.1, and 6.1 within a range of ± .001 at the .01 level of confidence, following procedures outlined in Hubert M. Blalock, Jr., *Social Statistics* (New York: McGraw-Hill, 1960), pp. 60–63, 165–67. The mean of the actual sample sizes was 3,162—between four and five times the estimated size needed for a random sample. The following speakers and documents are those sampled in the first session of the Twelfth Congress: *Annals of Congress*, House Foreign Relations Committee, 11/29/11: 374–77; Peter B. Porter, 12/6/11: 414–17; Felix Grundy, 12/9/11: 422–27; Richard M. Johnson, 12/11/11: 456–67; Robert Wright, 12/11/11: 467–75; John C. Calhoun, 12/12/11: 476–83; Henry Clay, 12/31/11: 596–602; and House Foreign Relations Committee, 6/25/12: 1546–54.

7. Table 4.4, "Mean Proportions for Association of Themes in 1812" (based on the documents sampled from the first session of the Twelfth Congress), illustrates typical levels of association and the meaningfulness of the .10 criterion used in this study to determine primary associations reported in Table 4.3. Of the 179 associations, 72.6 percent were at .049 or lower; 18.4 percent were between .050 and .099; 4.5 percent were between .100 and .149; 1.7 percent were between .150 and .199; 1.7 percent were between .200 and .249; and 1.1 percent were between .250 and .299. Therefore, only 9 percent met the .10 criterion. Additionally, a two-tailed test for the significance of a proportion indicates that only two of the primary associations in Table 4.3 fall below p<.05 (IC10>IA1 and IC10>IC5). Neither of these linkages figure prominently in the analysis of war themes and theme linkages. All but one other linkage (IC7>IC5) are significant at p<.01 or better, following the procedures outlined in James L. Bruning and B. L. Kintz, *Computational Handbook of Statistics* (Glenview, Ill.: Scott, Foresman, 1968), pp. 197–98.

8. Norman K. Risjord, "1812: Conservatives, War Hawks, and the Nation's Honor," *William and Mary Quarterly*, 3d ser., 18 (1961): 200.

9. James R. Andrews, "They Chose the Sword: Appeals to War in Nineteenth-Century American Public Address," *Today's Speech* 17 (1969): 4.

10. Larry James Winn, "The 'War Hawks' Call to Arms: Appeals for a Second War with Great Britain," *Southern Speech Communication Journal* 37 (1972): 408.

11. *Annals of Congress*, 12th Cong., 1st sess.: 1554.

12. Ibid., Richard M. Johnson: 459; John C. Calhoun: 482; Felix Grundy: 424–25.

13. Ibid., John A. Harper: 655–56.

14. Ibid., House Foreign Relations Committee: 1554.

15. Chaim Perelman and L. Olbrechts-Tyteca, *The New Rhetoric: A Treatise on Argumentation*, trans. John Wilkinson and Purcell Weaver (Notre Dame: Univ. of Notre Dame Press, 1969), pp. 294, 301–2.

16. Quincy Wright, *A Study of War*, 2d ed. (Chicago: Univ. of Chicago Press, 1965), p. 1086.

17. *Annals of Congress*, 12th Cong., 1st sess., House Committee on Foreign Relations: 376.

18. Ibid., Madison: 13.

19. Ibid., House Committee on Foreign Relations: 374; Peter B. Porter: 415.

20. Ibid., Richard M. Johnson: 457; House Committee on Foreign Relations: 1546.

21. Ibid., House Committee on Foreign Relations: 1554.

22. Ibid.: 376.

23. Ibid., Samuel McKee: 507–8.

24. Ibid.: 508.

25. Ibid., Madison: 11.

26. Ibid., House Committee on Foreign Relations: 1552.

27. Ibid.

28. Ibid., Madison: 1624; Henry Clay: 601.

29. Ibid., Joseph Desha: 487.

30. Ibid., House Committee on Foreign Relations: 375; Peter B. Porter: 414.

31. "To _____," 18 June 1812, *The Papers of Henry Clay*, ed. James F. Hopkins, 5 vols. (Lexington: Univ. of Kentucky Press, 1959), I: 674; see also "To Jesse Bledsoe," 18 June 1812, p. 675. "Speech Urging Passage of the Embargo Bill," 1 April 1812, *Papers of Henry Clay*, I: 642.

32. *Annals of Congress*, 12th Cong., 1st sess., Peter B. Porter: 415.

33. Thomas Jefferson to William Duane, 20 April 1812, Jefferson Papers, Library of Congress.

34. *Annals of Congress*, 12th Cong., 1st sess., Joseph Desha: 484.

35. Ibid., Jonathan Roberts: 503.

36. Ibid., John C. Calhoun: 476, 482.

37. William Jones to Jonathan Roberts, 10 June 1812, William Jones Papers, Uselma Clark Smith Collection, Historical Society of Pennsylvania.

38. Jonathan Roberts Memoirs, vol. 2, pp. 10, 19, Historical Society of Pennsylvania.

39. Thomas Gholson to _____, 1812 (fragment), Brunswick Co., Va. (Acc. 3307-a), University of Virginia.

40. Clyde E. Reeves, "The Debates on the War of 1812: Parliament and Congress Compared," Ph.D. diss., University of Illinois, 1958, pp. 74–75.

41. *Annals of Congress*, 12th Cong., 1st sess., Daniel Sheffey: 621.

42. Ibid., "Address of the Minority to their Constituents": 2200, 2202.

43. Ibid., John Randolph: 534, 441.

44. Ibid., "Address of the Minority to their Constituents": 2207.

45. Ibid., Daniel Sheffey: 625.

46. Ibid., "Address of the Minority to their Constituents": 2198.

47. Ibid., Henry Clay: 599.
48. Ibid., John C. Calhoun: 479.
49. Ibid., Daniel Sheffey: 626.
50. Ibid., Daniel Sheffey: 623; John Randolph: 533.
51. Ibid., Daniel Sheffey: 626.
52. John Randolph to James M. Garnett, 1 February 1812, Garnett-Randolph Papers (Acc. 1883), University of Virginia.
53. Kurt W. Ritter and James R. Andrews, *The American Ideology: Reflections of the Revolution in American Rhetoric* (Falls Church, Va.: Speech Communication Association, 1978), pp. 6–12, argue that the strategy of American revolutionaries was to degrade the British by representing them as "literally and figuratively raping America." This was taken as a symptom of the moral decline of England and was designed to "wean colonists from old affections" and "to construct an image of America totally independent from (and superior to) Great Britain." Americans had learned to suspect England's motives. John Adams wrote in 1795, for example, that Britain's "commercial hostilities" were designed "not so much to increase their own wealth, ships, or sailors, as the diminution of ours. A jealousy of our naval power is the true motive, the real passion which actuates them; they consider the United States as their rival, and the most dangerous rival they have in the world." Reported in Frank A. Updyke, *The Diplomacy of the War of 1812* (Baltimore: Johns Hopkins Univ. Press, 1915), p. 2. Irving Brant, *James Madison: The President, 1809–1812* (Indianapolis: Bobbs Merrill, 1956), p. 77, also reports that Madison held similar suspicions in the summer of 1809. He felt that Britain's "object is not to retaliate injury to an enemy; but to prevent the legitimate trade of the United States from interfering with the London smugglers of sugar and coffee."
54. Resolutions of Citizens' Meeting, 19 May 1812, Norristown, Montgomery County, Historical Society of Pennsylvania.

Chapter Five

1. Peter Shaw, "The War of 1812 Could Not Take Place," *Yale Review* 62 (1973): 544–56.
2. Henry Adams, *A History of the United States During the Administrations of Jefferson and Madison*, 4 vols. (1891–96; rpt. ed., New York: Albert and Charles Boni, 1930), IV, Book 9: 139–40.
3. Rudolph M. Bell, *Faction and Party in American Politics: The House of Representatives, 1789–1801* (Westport, Ct.: Greenwood, 1973), p. 180.
4. Ibid., pp. 155–81. Cohesion indexes available upon request.
5. C. F. Adams, "The Life of John Adams" in *The Works of John Adams*, ed. C. F. Adams, 9 vols. (1850–56; rpt. ed., Freeport, N.Y.: Books for Libraries Press, 1969), I: 575; Gilbert Chinard, *Honest John Adams* (Boston: Little, Brown, 1933), pp. 264–78; and Stephen G. Kurtz, *The Presidency of John Adams: The Collapse of Federalism, 1795–1800* (Philadelphia: Univ. of Pennsylvania Press, 1957), p. 311.
6. Page Smith, *John Adams*, 2 vols. (Garden City, N.Y.: Doubleday, 1962), II: 979; Ralph Adams Brown, *The Presidency of John Adams* (Lawrence, Ks.: Univ. Press of Kansas, 1975), p. 58; Bell, *Party and Faction*, p. 175; Richard Buel, Jr., *Securing the Revolution: Ideology in American Politics 1798–1815* (Ithaca: Cornell Univ. Press, 1972); Albert H. Bowman, *The Struggle for Neutrality: Franco-American Diplomacy During the Federalist Era* (Knoxville: Univ. of Tennessee Press, 1974), pp. 306–33, 361; and Daniel M. Sisson, *The Revolution of 1800* (New York: Alfred A. Knopf, 1974), chapter 6.
7. Scales available upon request.

8. Alexander DeConde, *The Quasi-War: The Politics and Diplomacy of the Undeclared War with France, 1797–1801* (New York: Charles Scribner's Sons, 1966), pp. 105–6, makes the same point.

9. See Alexander Hamilton, *The Works of Alexander Hamilton*, ed. John C. Hamilton, 7 vols. (New York: J. F. Trow, 1850–51), vol. VI, and George Gibbs, ed., *Memoirs of the Administrations of Washington and John Adams, Edited from the Papers of Oliver Wolcott, Secretary of the Treasury*, 2 vols. (New York: W. Van Norden, 1846), vol. II.

10. John Adams to Benjamin Lincoln, 10 March 1800. *Works of Adams*, IX: 47. Kurtz, *Presidency of John Adams*, pp. 269–82; Brown, *Presidency of John Adams*, pp. 26–27; Chinard, *Honest John Adams*, pp. 262, 285; Kaplan, *Colonies into Nation: American Diplomacy, 1763–1801* (New York: Macmillan, 1972), p. 262.

11. Peter Shaw, *The Character of John Adams* (Chapel Hill: Univ. of North Carolina Press, 1976), pp. 254, 252.

12. The precipitating incident for Smith's removal was Treasury Secretary Albert Gallatin's threatened resignation. Albert Gallatin to James Madison [March 1811], in Henry Adams, ed., *The Writings of Albert Gallatin*, 2 vols. (Philadelphia: J. B. Lippincott, 1879), I: 495. For Madison's reasons, see "Memorandum as to Robert Smith," Madison Papers, Library of Congress or in Gailliard Hunt, ed., *The Writings of James Madison*, 9 vols. (New York: G. P. Putnam's Sons, 1908), VIII: 138 and this book, chapter 2.

13. See chapter 2.

14. Shaw, *Character of John Adams*, p. 261.

15. *Annals of Congress*, 5th Cong., 1st sess.: 54–59; 5th Cong., 3d sess.: 2420–22; 6th Cong., 1st sess.: 188–90.

16. Ibid., 5th Cong., 2d sess.: 631.

17. Ibid., 1271–72.

18. Ibid., 1594, 1870, 1972, and 2029.

19. Especially influential during the summer of 1798 was Hamilton's attempt to be appointed second in command of the army. See Adams, *Works*, VIII: 573–606.

20. For a good comparison between the Jefferson and Madison Congresses and Federalist Congresses, see Joseph Cooper, "Jeffersonian Attitudes Toward Executive Leadership and Committee Development in the House of Representative, 1789–1829," *Western Political Quarterly* 18 (1965): 45–63.

21. For a discussion of the method of theme analysis employed, see chapter 4, pp. 40–44 and nn. 6, 7, and 8. The following speeches were sampled: *Annals of Congress*, 5th Cong., 2d sess., John Allen, 4/20/98: 1476–88; Robert Goodloe Harper, 4/18/98: 1445–53; Harrison G. Otis, 4/20/98: 1488–94; Samuel W. Dana, 4/20/98: 1501–5; and Samuel Sitgreaves, 5/11/98: 1685–89 and 6/12/98: 1901–3.

22. *Annals of Congress*, 5th Cong., 2d sess., Dana: 1501; Otis: 1261; Harper: 1450; and Adams: 631–32.

23. Ibid., Otis: 1261.

24. Ibid., Harper: 1344–45, 1748.

25. *Annals of Congress*, 5th Cong., 1st sess., William Smith: 87.

26. Ibid., Dennis: 158.

27. *Annals of Congress*, 5th Cong., 2d sess., Sewall: 1327.

28. Noble E. Cunningham, Jr., ed., *Circular Letters of Congressmen to Their Constituents, 1789–1829*, 3 vols. (Chapel Hill: Univ. of North Carolina Press, 1978), I: 151. Letter dated 10 February 1799. Also p. 172 for letter dated 20 March 1799.

29. *Annals of Congress*, 5th Cong., 2d sess., Otis: 1988.

30. Ibid., 5th Cong., 1st sess., William Smith: 86–87.

31. Cunningham, ed., *Circular Letters*, Harper, 23 July 1798, p. 142; 10 February 1799, pp. 149–150; *Annals of Congress*, 5th Cong., 2d sess., Allen: 1478, 1480; Cunningham, ed.,

Circular Letters, I, Harper, 20 March 1799, p. 172; and *Annals of Congress*, 5th Cong., 2d sess., Harper: 1748–49.

32. *Annals of Congress*, 5th Cong., 2d sess., Otis: 1988.

33. Ibid., Allen: 1482.

34. Ibid., Otis: 2017, 1961–62.

35. Ibid., Harper: 1992.

36. For additional examples, see Cunningham, ed., *Circular Letters*, I, Harper, 23 July 1798, pp. 139–42; 20 March 1799, pp. 166–72; and 10 February 1799, pp. 149–50.

37. Michael Osborn, "Archetypal Metaphor in Rhetoric: The Light-Dark Family," *Quarterly Journal of Speech* 53 (1967): 115, 119–20, 125.

38. James Watson to Joel Barlow, 26 October 1798, in Gibbs, ed., *Memoirs*, II: 112–13, 115.

39. Stephen Higginson to Timothy Pickering, 9 June 1798, 3 March 1799, 24 November 1799, and 31 January 1799, in J. Franklin Jameson, ed., "Letters of Stephen Higginson, 1783–1804," *Annual Report of the American Historical Association for the Year 1896* (Washington, 1897), pp. 808, 819–20, 831, and 818.

40. These are the thoughts of Sedgwick paraphrased by Richard E. Welch, Jr., *Theodore Sedgwick, Federalist: A Political Portrait* (Middletown, Ct.: Wesleyan Univ. Press, 1965), pp. 167–68. Robert G. Harper, *Observations on the Dispute Between the United States and France* (Philadelphia: Philanthropia Press, 1797), p. 157. George Cabot to Wolcott, 26 March 1798, and 25 October 1798, in Gibbs, ed., *Memoirs*, II: 43, 109.

41. *Annals of Congress*, 5th Cong., 2d sess., Claiborne: 1882; Giles: 1348, 1339, 1323; N. Smith: 1699–1700.

42. Morton Borden, *The Federalism of James A. Bayard* (New York: Columbia Univ. Press, 1955), pp. 23–24; and Lance Banning, *The Jeffersonian Persuasion: Evolution of a Party Ideology* (Ithaca: Cornell Univ. Press, 1978), ch. 9.

43. Alexander DeConde, *The Quasi-War: The Politics and Diplomacy of the Undeclared War with France, 1797–1801* (New York: Charles Scribner's Sons, 1966), pp. 4–6, 14, 107, 331–32.

44. John R. Howe, *The Changing Political Thought of John Adams* (Princeton: Princeton Univ. Press, 1966), pp. 232–40.

45. Richard Hofstadter, *The Idea of a Party System: The Rise of Legitimate Opposition in the United States, 1780–1840* (Berkeley and Los Angeles: Univ. of California Press, 1969).

46. John Adams to Thomas Jefferson, 2 February 1817, in Lester J. Cappon, ed., *The Adams-Jefferson Letters: The Complete Correspondence Between Thomas Jefferson and Abigail and John Adams*, 2 vols. (Chapel Hill: Univ. of North Carolina Press, 1959), II: 508.

Chapter Six

1. In Thomas A. Bailey, *Presidential Greatness: The Image and the Man from George Washington to the Present* (New York: Appleton-Century, 1966), pp. 24–25.

2. Noble E. Cunningham, Jr., *The Process of Government under Jefferson* (Princeton: Princeton Univ. Press, 1978), p. 12.

3. Ibid., pp. 316, 323.

4. Robert M. Johnstone, Jr., *Jefferson and the Presidency: Leadership in the Young Republic* (Ithaca: Cornell Univ. Press, 1978), pp. 14, 43, 46, 85–97.

5. Ibid., pp. 160, 251–305.

6. Burton Spivak, *Jefferson's English Crisis: Commerce, Embargo, and the Republican Revolution* (Charlottesville: Univ. Press of Virginia, 1979); Spivak, "Republican Dreams

and National Interest: The Jeffersonians and American Foreign Policy," *SHAFR Newsletter* XII (1981): 1.

7. Spivak, "Republican Dreams," pp. 6–7.

8. Spivak, *English Crisis*, pp. 72–98; ibid., pp. 9, 14–16.

9. Drew R. McCoy, *The Elusive Republic: Political Economy in Jeffersonian America* (Chapel Hill: Univ. of North Carolina Press, 1980), esp. pp. 185–238, quotes on pp. 188, 210, 235.

10. Fred E. Fiedler and Martin M. Chemers, *Leadership and Effective Management* (Glenview, Ill.: Scott, Foresman, 1974), pp. 63–64 ff.

11. Dumas Malone, *Jefferson the President: Second Term, 1805–1809* (Boston: Little, Brown, 1974), p. 439.

12. Spivak, *English Crisis*, pp. 72–98 for *Chesapeake*, pp. 222–24 for Burr.

13. Thomas Jefferson to Tench Coxe, 27 March 1807. In *The Writings of Thomas Jefferson*, Andrew A. Lipscomb and Albert E. Bergh, eds., 20 vols. (Washington: The Thomas Jefferson Memorial Assn., 1903–4), XI: 175.

14. Thomas Jefferson to William Branch Giles, 20 April 1807, ibid., pp. 187–91; Thomas Jefferson to George Hay, 2 June 1807, ibid., pp. 213–16. By September, the link between the British and Burr became explicit in Jefferson's letters. "[Burr] is preserved to become the rallying point of all the disaffected and the worthless of the United States, and to be the pivot on which all the intrigues and the conspiracies which foreign governments may wish to disturb us with, are to turn." Thomas Jefferson to George Hay, 4 September 1807. Ibid., pp. 360–61.

15. Thomas Jefferson to James Bowdoin, 10 July 1807, ibid., p. 269.

16. Thomas Jefferson to Craven Peyton, 10 August 1807, in Spivak, *English Crisis*, p. 72.

17. Bradford Perkins, *Prologue to War: England and the United States, 1805–1812* (Berkeley and Los Angeles: Univ. of California Press, 1961), pp. 149, 153; Spivak, *English Crisis*, p. 74.

18. Thomas Jefferson to Madison, 20 August 1807, *Writings*, XI: 340–1 (emphasis added).

19. R. L. Hatzenbuehler and R. L. Ivie, "Justifying the War of 1812: Toward a Model of Congressional Behavior in Early War Crises," *Social Science History* 4 (1980), 460–61.

20. Thomas Jefferson to Robert Smith, 8 October 1807, *Writings*: XI: 377, Spivak, *English Crisis*, p. 89.

21. Thomas Jefferson to William H. Cabell, 1 November 1807, *Writings*, XI, 388–89. Richard Mannix, "Gallatin, Jefferson, and the Embargo of 1808," *Diplomatic History* 3 (1979): 151–72.

22. The method used to analyze themes is explained in chapter 4, pp. 40–44 and notes 6–8. The following speeches were sampled: *Annals of Congress*, 10th Cong., 1st sess., Richard M. Johnson, 12/11/07: 1151–56 and 4/12/08: 2087–91; William A. Burwell, 4/5/08: 1954–59 and 4/11/08: 2073–75; James Fisk, 4/13/08: 2110–18; George W. Campbell, 4/6/08: 2006–21; and John Love, 4/13/08: 2092–2108.

23. Compare Table 6.1 with Table 5.3.

24. *Annals of Congress*, 10th Cong., 1st sess., Johnson: 1155.

25. Ibid., Love: 2096.

26. Ibid., Campbell: 2014.

27. Ibid., Key: 2123.

28. Ibid., Williams: 2136.

29. Ibid., Johnson: 2090.

30. Larry James Winn, "The War Hawks' Call to Arms: Appeals for a Second War with Great Britain," *Southern Speech Communication Journal*, 37 (1972), 408.

31. *Annals of Congress*, 10th Cong., 1st sess., Fisk: 2116.

32. Ibid., Campbell: 2139, 975.

33. Ibid., Rhea: 1663.

34. Ibid., Newton: 1665.

35. Burwell Bassett to Joseph Prentis, 25 February 1808, Webb-Prentis Collection (Acc. 4136, Box 2), University of Virginia.

36. *Annals of Congress*, 10th Cong., 1st sess., Campbell: 2016.

37. Desha, circular letter, 29 March 1808, p. 544 in Noble E. Cunningham, Jr., ed., *Circular Letters of Congressmen to Their Constituents, 1789–1829*, 3 vols., (Chapel Hill: Univ. of North Carolina Press, 1978), II: 544.

38. Johnson, circular letter, 10 April 1808, ibid., II: 552.

39. *Annals of Congress*, 10th Cong., 1st sess., Fisk: 2117.

40. Desha, circular letter, 29 March 1808, in Cunningham, *Circular Letters*, II: 541.

41. *Annals of Congress*, 10th Cong., 1st sess., Eppes: 2045.

42. Ibid., Campbell: 975, 2013–14, and 2017–18.

43. Ibid., Newton: 1664, 1665–67.

44. Ibid., Rhea: 1663.

45. Thomas Jefferson to William Duane, 28 March 1811, Jefferson Papers, Library of Congress.

46. Thomas Jefferson to John Adams, 11 June 1812, in Lester J. Cappon, ed., *The Adams-Jefferson Letters: The Complete Correspondence Between Thomas Jefferson and Abigail and John Adams*, 2 vols. (Chapel Hill: Univ. of North Carolina Press, 1959), II: 308.

Chapter Seven

1. For the latest debate concerning the embargo's authorship and implementation, compare Richard Mannix, "Gallatin, Jefferson, and the Embargo of 1808," *Diplomatic History* 3 (1979): 151–72 and Burton Spivak, *Jefferson's English Crisis: Commerce, Embargo, and the Republican Revolution* (Charlottesville: Univ. Press of Virginia, 1979).

2. Spivak, *Jefferson's English Crisis*, p. 197; Bradford Perkins, *Prologue to War: England and the United States, 1805–1812* (Berkeley and Los Angeles: Univ. of California Press, 1961), p. 182; Roger H. Brown, *The Republic in Peril, 1812* (New York: Columbia Univ. Press, 1964), pp. 20–21.

3. An index of 50 is operationally used as a basis of comparison. See chapter 3, n. 16, p. 148.

4. Thomas Jefferson to Thomas Mann Randolph, 7 February 1809; Jefferson to Alexander McRae, 8 February 1809. Jefferson Papers, Library of Congress.

5. Thomas Jefferson to Henry Dearborn, 16 July 1810. Ibid.

6. Spivak, *Jefferson's English Crisis*, p. 184. Walter Wilson Jennings also emphasizes Adams's role in the embargo's repeal in *The American Embargo, 1807–1809, with Particular Reference to its Effects on Industry* (Iowa City: Univ. of Iowa Press, 1921), pp. 163–65.

7. *Annals of Congress*, 10th Cong., 2d sess.: 941–42; 976–77.

8. Ibid.: 1048; 1078–79; 1095, 980.

9. Ibid.: 132–38.

10. Ezekiel Bacon to Joseph Story, 22 January 1809. Joseph Story Papers, Library of Congress.

11. Bacon to Story, 26 February 1809. Ibid.

12. We are using the word "predictive" in a descriptive rather than a statistical way. The value of Table 7.3 lies in confirming Bacon's position that the naval issue is a behavioral link between embargo and war (Table 7.7).

13. Ezekiel Bacon, *An Address, Delivered Before the Republican Citizens of Berkshire, Assembled at Pittsfield, to Celebrate the Thirty-Fourth Anniversary of American Independence, July 4, 1810* (Pittsfield, Mass.: Phinehas Allen, 1810), pp. 15, 20–22.

14. Ibid., pp. 12–13. This address convinces us of the consistency of Bacon's position, i.e., trying to build a moderate position between commercial restriction and war. William Barlow and David O. Powell do not appear to have consulted this document and, on the basis of their examination of Bacon's voting and letters to Story, conclude that "he was less than consistent on the subject of when and whether warlike measures should follow the embargo's repeal." (See n. 35 also.) Barlow and Powell, "Congressman Ezekiel Bacon of Massachusetts and the Coming of the War of 1812," *Historical Journal of Western Massachusetts* 6 (1978): 31.

15. Federalists unanimously favored the embargo's repeal in the extreme in every part of the country except the South and West where two members of the Federalist bloc out of 8 (25 percent) opposed its repeal in the extreme. The 34 "unwavering" Federalist votes become important, however, only when they are combined with the Northern Republicans and the Republican moderates. In other words, the Federalist argument that appears in numerous letters from the session that they had effected the embargo's repeal by their persistent opposition simply was not the case. As examples of these letters, see Timothy Pitkin, Jr. to John Treadwell, 31 January 1809. John Treadwell Papers, Connecticut Historical Society; and Benjamin Tallmadge to Tapping Reeve, 27 February 1809. Tapping Reeve Papers, Yale University Library.

16. *Annals of Congress*, 10th Cong., 2d sess.: 1498; 1450; 1278–88; 1443–47; 1510–11; 1251–14. See also William A. Burwell's circular letter to his constituents, 27 February 1809, in Noble E. Cunningham, Jr., ed., *Circular Letters of Congressmen to Their Constituents, 1789–1829*, 3 vols., (Chapel Hill: Univ. of North Carolina Press, 1978), II: 649. Also Wilson Cary Nicholas's circular, [March] 1809, pp. 670–71.

17. Lyon was a renegade Republican who often embarrassed his more "predictable" colleagues. One candid Republican reacted to his reelection to Congress in 1808 thus: "I regret exceedingly that it is not in my power to confirm to you the success which I anticipated in relation to our Congressional election: *Lyon* has triumphed owing to the division of the Republican votes between New & Work. . . . It would have afforded me great pleasure to see the old man left at home to attend his store, and next to that I am rejoiced to see that nearly 2/3 of the District preferred another candidate, and I beg you to bear this in mind, and should he vapour next winter at Washington upon his re-election and thereby presume a coincidence in sentiment between himself and the District he *misrepresents*, let the fact declared at the poll refute the calumny." A. Butler to G. W. Campbell, 15 September 1808. G. W. Campbell Papers, Library of Congress.

18. John Love to Robert Smith, 23 December 1808. Thomas Newton to Robert Smith, 23 December 1808, and 1 February 1809, Virginia Letters (Acc. 5736), University of Virginia.

19. Thomas Newton to John Tyler, Sr., 26 December 1808. Executive Papers of Governor John Tyler, Sr. (Box 158), Virginia State Library.

20. Thomas Jefferson to Levi Lincoln, 13 November 1808. Jefferson Papers, Library of Congress.

21. On November 15, 1808, Albert Gallatin wrote to Jefferson to convey his and Madison's beliefs that the Congress should be given "some precise & distinct course. As to what that should be we may not all perfectly agree, and perhaps the knowledge of the various feelings of the members & of the apparent public opinion may on consideration induce a revision of our own. I feel myself nearly as undetermined between enforcing the embargo or war as I was on our last meetings. But I think that we must (or rather you must) decide the question absolutely, so that we may point out a decisive course either way to our friends." Jefferson Papers, Library of Congress. Then on December 29, 1808, Gallatin wrote to Joseph H. Nicholson,

"Never was I so overwhelmed with public business. That would be nothing if we went right. But a great confusion and perplexity reigns in Congress. Mr. Madison is, as I always knew him, slow in taking his ground, but firm when the story arises. What I had foreseen has taken place. A majority will not adhere to the embargo much longer; and if war be not speedily determined on, submission will soon ensue." *The Writings of Albert Gallatin*, ed. Henry Adams, 2 vols. (Philadelphia: J. B. Lippincott, 1879), I: 449. See also James Madison's letter to William Pinkney, 11 February 1809: "You will see with regret the difficulty experienced in collecting the mind of Congress into some proper focus. On no occasion were the ideas so unstable and so scattered." In Perkins, *Prologue to War*, p. 226. On the practical problems with the strategy of choosing between embargo and war, see Wilson Cary Nicholas's circular letter, [March] 1809, in Cunningham, *Circular Letters*, II: 672.

22. Reginald C. Stuart, "James Madison and the Militants: Republican Disunity and Replacing the Embargo," *Diplomatic History* 6 (1982): 145–67. See also Stuart's *War and American Thought: From the Revolution to the Monroe Doctrine* (Kent: Kent State University Press, 1982).

23. Ibid., p. 158.

24. *Annals of Congress*, 11th Cong., 2d sess.: 1225; 1254 ff.

25. Ibid.: 1403–4; 1445; 1463; Eppes: 1487–93; 2021–28; Burwell: 1487; 1559–60; 2021–28; 2051–53.

26. Ibid., 11 Cong., 3d sess.: 1098.

27. Ibid., 11 Cong., 1st sess.: 155–56.

28. Ibid., 11 Cong., 2d sess., Dana: 1490; Quincy: 1493. Donald R. Hickey argues that the Federalists "never wavered in their support of maritime defense, in peace or in war. Always the maritime party, they had tried in early 1812 to limit the war to a defensive maritime contest in the tradition of 1798." Neither the votes nor the speeches of Federalists in the Eleventh Congress support such a conclusion. D. R. Hickey, "Federalist Party Unity and the War of 1812," *Journal of American Studies* 12 (1978): 30–31.

29. *Annals of Congress*, 12th Cong., 1st sess.: 553–56.

30. Ibid.: 803.

31. Ibid., Bassett: 859–66; Mitchill: 866–75; Lowndes: 895; Nelson: 991–94.

32. Ibid., Seybert: 823–33; McKee: 970–76; Johnson: 875–84; Roberts: 899–907; Smilie: 910; Fisk: 968–70; Bibb: 977–91.

33. Extreme positions on the naval and war scales are reported in R. L. Hatzenbuehler, "The War Hawks and the Question of Congressional Leadership in 1812," *Pacific Historical Review* 45 (1976): 5–6. Ninety-two percent of the extremists on both issues in Table 7.3 were *Northerners* (11 of 12) whereas 56 percent of the extremists on both issues in Table 7.7 were *Southerners* (9 of 16).

34. For a discussion of the War Hawks of 1812, see Hatzenbuehler, ibid. and "Letter to the Editor," *Pacific Historical Review* 45 (1976): 644–45.

35. John Randolph reported in April 1812 that "[Peter B.] Porter our chairman of F[oreign] R[elations] is gone—completely broken down, and Bacon (as the auctioneers say) is going! going!" Randolph to James M. Garnett 14 April 1812, Garnett-Randolph Papers (Acc. 1883), University of Virginia. Barlow and Powell erroneously conclude that Bacon's opposition to the navy shows him as "a doctrinaire, strict-constructionist, anti-navy 'Old Republican' who even in the face of impending war refused to compromise the 'Principles of 1798.' " Instead, it shows how he had been stripped of the only hope for a solution to his nation's problems short of war. Barlow and Powell, "Congressman Ezekiel Bacon," p. 33.

Chapter Eight

1. Quincy Wright, *A Study of War*, 2d ed. (Chicago: Univ. of Chicago Press, 1965), pp. 1083–84, 1086, 1095, and 1103. Wright draws upon Harold D. Lasswell's analysis of major themes in war propaganda, *Propaganda Technique in the World War* (New York: Alfred A. Knopf, 1927), especially chapters 3 and 4.

2. Kenneth Burke, *Permanence and Change* (1954; rpt. Indianapolis: Bobbs-Merrill, 1965), pp. 284–85. See also Kenneth Burke, "Dramatism," in *Communication: Concepts and Perspectives*, ed. Lee Thayer (Washington, D.C.: Spartan Books, 1967), p. 342.

3. Hugh Dalziel Duncan, *Communication and Social Order* (London: Oxford Univ. Press, 1962), pp. 129–35.

4. Robert L. Ivie, "Images of Savagery in American Justifications for War," *Communication Monographs* 47 (1980): 279–94.

5. Bradford Perkins, *Prologue to War: England and the United States, 1805–1812* (Berkeley and Los Angeles: Univ. of California Press, 1961), p. 3. See also Reginald Horsman, *The Causes of the War of 1812* (Philadelphia: Univ. of Pennsylvania Press, 1962), p. 14. In Horsman's judgment, "Actually what is really surprising is not that America declared war on England in 1812, but that she had not done so several years earlier. In many ways it is easier to show why America should have gone to war in 1807 or 1809 rather than in 1812."

6. Perkins, ibid., pp. vii–viii, 300, 418; and Norman K. Risjord, "1812: Conservatives, War Hawks, and the Nation's Honor," *William and Mary Quarterly*, 3d ser., 18 (1961): 196. Perkins, p. 99, also stresses that, although "tangible pressures played a fundamental part in the coming of war," the nation still could prosper "despite foreign interference." In fact, he emphasizes, "it is most important to recognize the moral implications of the challenges America faced. Britain treated the new republic as if Yorktown had been an incomplete victory. To many . . . independence seemed almost a dream."

7. Risjord, "1812: Conservatives, War Hawks, and the Nation's Honor," p. 200.

8. Roger H. Brown, *The Republic in Peril: 1812* (New York: Columbia Univ. Press, 1964), p. 73.

9. Risjord, "1812: Conservatives, War Hawks, and the Nation's Honor," p. 200.

10. See chapter 4.

11. See Brown, *Republic in Peril*, chapter 4.

12. *Annals of Congress*, 11th Cong., 2d sess., Sawyer: 1299.

13. Ibid., Desha: 1301, 1304, 1312.

14. Ibid., Garland: 1782–83.

15. *Annals of Congress*, 10th Cong., 2d sess., Johnson: 582, 586–87.

16. Ibid., Jackson: 635, 637, 640, 653–54, 655, 656, and 660.

17. Noble E. Cunningham, Jr., ed., *Circular Letters of Congressmen to Their Constituents, 1789–1829*, 3 vols., (Chapel Hill: Univ. of North Carolina Press, 1978), II: 625, 627.

18. Ibid., p. 621.

19. Andrew Gregg to Samuel Stewart, 22 December 1809, Gregg Collection, Library of Congress.

20. *Annals of Congress*, 11th Cong., 2d sess., Desha: 1301–2, 1304–5, 1309, 1311-12.

21. Ibid., Bibb: 1342–43, 1346, 1348–49.

22. Ibid., Taylor: 1639; Gholson: 1690; Taylor: 1716, 1776.

23. Ibid., Taylor: 1776.

24. Ibid., Taylor: 1780.

25. *Annals of Congress*, 11th Cong., 2d sess., Gholson: 1772–73.

26. Ibid., Boyd: 1684.

27. Andrew Gregg to William Jones, 8 April 1810; William Jones Papers, Uselma Clarke Smith Collection; Historical Society of Pennsylvania.

28. Ezekiel Bacon to Joseph Story, 22 October 1810; Joseph Story Papers, Library of Congress.

29. *Annals of Congress*, 11th Cong., 3d sess., Cheves: 884.

30. Ibid., Rhea: 893–94.

31. Ibid., Cheves: 887.

32. Ibid., Wright: 952, 955.

33. Horsman, *Causes of the War of 1812*, p. 178.

34. *Annals of Congress*, 11th Cong., 3d sess., Cheves: 886.

35. Brown, *Republic in Peril*, p. 38.

Chapter Nine

1. Robert E. Shalhope, "Republicanism and Early American Historiography," *William and Mary Quarterly*, 3d ser., 39 (1982): 334–56; Bernard Bailyn, "The Central Themes of the American Revolution: An Interpretation," in Stephen G. Kurtz and James H. Hutson, eds., *Essays on the American Revolution* (Chapel Hill: Univ. of North Carolina Press, 1973), p. 19.

2. Kenneth Burke, *Permanence and Change: An Anatomy of Purpose*, 2d ed. (1954; rpt. ed., Indianapolis: Bobbs-Merrill, 1965), p. 107.

3. Patricia Watlington, *The Partisan Spirit: Kentucky Politics, 1779–1792* (New York: Atheneum, 1972); Jackson Turner Main, *Political Parties Before the Constitution* (Chapel Hill: Univ. of North Carolina Press, 1973); Ronald P. Formisano, "Deferential-Participant Politics: The Early Republic's Political Culture, 1789–1840," *American Political Science Review* 68 (1974): 473–87. See also Ronald P. Formisano, *The Transformation of Political Culture: Massachusetts Parties, 1790s–1840s* (New York: Oxford Univ. Press, 1983), esp. chapter 7.

4. Shalhope, "Republicanism and Early American Historiography," p. 356.

5. A good statement of Burke's perspective toward symbolic action is provided in his "Definition of Man," *Language as Symbolic Action: Essays on Life, Literature, and Method* (Berkeley and Los Angeles: Univ. of California Press, 1968), pp. 3–24.

6. Shalhope, "Republicanism and Early American Historiography," p. 351.

Bibliographical Essay

The research of three scholars writing in the 1960s has had a substantial impact on our work. Norman K. Risjord's article, "1812: Conservatives, War Hawks, and the Nation's Honor," *William and Mary Quarterly*, 3d ser., 18 (1961): 196–210, was especially valuable because it shifted research on the political origins of the War of 1812 from sectional and economic origins of the war to ideological motivations. Contemporaneously, Bradford Perkins's study of British and American relations prior to the war, *Prologue to War: England and the United States, 1805–1812* (Berkeley and Los Angeles: Univ. of California Press, 1961), integrated domestic political considerations into diplomatic exchanges between the two countries. One conclusion to be drawn from both studies was that the actions of people, not some deterministic sequence of forces, brought on the war. Roger H. Brown's book, *The Republic in Peril: 1812* (New York: Columbia Univ. Press, 1964), added to this growing emphasis on ideas and decision making a behavioral dimension which focused on Republican partisanship as a key to the movement toward war. In addition to shaping much of the research of scholars in the last two decades and a great deal of our thinking, these same three scholars ferreted out the relevant manuscript collections and highlighted what the advocates of war said in justification of their actions. Their careful readings of these sources have been a constant check on whether we were really saying anything new.

With regard to the literature on Adams's administration, Stephen G. Kurtz's negative observations on Adams's style of leadership and problems as president published twenty-five years ago—that Adams could neither fill the void left by Washington's departure nor accommodate himself to Jefferson's democracy—still dominates treatments of the period (Stephen G. Kurtz, *The Presidency of John Adams: The Collapse of Federalism* [Philadelphia: Univ. of Pennsylvania Press, 1957]. Alexander De Conde's blend of politics and diplomacy, *The Quasi-War: The Politics and Diplomacy of the Undeclared War With France, 1797–1801* (New York: Charles Scribner's Sons, 1966), is still the best treatment of the problems Adams faced. Rudolph M. Bell's study of voting during the period, *Faction and Party in American Politics: The House of Representatives, 1789–1801* (Westport, Ct.: Greenwood, 1973) provides a good starting point from which to investigate congressional behavior, but his conclusions must be questioned based upon his definitions of partisan behavior. Adams's personality as it affected his political decisions is insightfully explored in Peter Shaw's psychological study of the man, *The Character of John Adams* (Chapel Hill: Univ. of North Carolina Press, 1976).

Jefferson's presidency also presents the scholar with a wealth of materials, but proper perspective is lacking. Overall, Forrest McDonald's book, *The Presidency of Thomas Jefferson* (Lawrence, Ks.: Univ. Press of Kansas, 1976), is the most instructive because it best balances the problems of the second term against the accomplishments of the first. For the philosophy and political implementation of economic coercion, see Drew R. McCoy, *The Elusive Republic: Political Economy in Jeffersonian America* (Chapel Hill: Univ. of North Carolina Press, 1979) and Burton Spivak, *Jefferson's English Crisis: Commerce, Embargo, and the Republican Revolution* (Charlottesville: Univ. Press of Virginia, 1979).

Madison, as Adams, has suffered by unfair comparisons with Jefferson. Noble E. Cunningham's recent administrative study, *The Process of Government Under Jefferson* (Princeton: Princeton Univ. Press, 1978), shows how Jefferson effectively used partisanship to control the Congress in his first term, but his conclusion that Madison failed to do so cannot be supported. The best antidote to this traditional view of Madison's presidency is to be found in J. C. A. Stagg's articles in the *William and Mary Quarterly* (3d ser.), "James Madison and the 'Malcontents': The Political Origins of the War of 1812," 33 (1976): 557–85 and "James Madison and the Coercion of Great Britain: Canada, the West Indies, and the War of 1812," 38 (1981): 3–34.

Another tendency of recent scholarship is to see Madison's presidency as forming the apex of the battle between "court and country" in American politics—see Lance G. Banning, *The Jeffersonian Persuasion: Evolution of a Party Ideology* (Ithaca: Cornell Univ. Press, 1978). Far too much emphasis is currently being placed on the supposed carry-over of British politics into the American experience. As Joyce Appleby recently pointed out in her article, "What Is Still American in the Political Philosophy of Thomas Jefferson?" *William and Mary Quarterly*, 3d ser., 39 (1982): 287–309, aspects of both court and country are apparent in each of the two major political parties of early America. It is also important to note that Federalists and Quids shared many of the Republicans' concerns over defending republicanism, a thesis developed with most effect by James M. Banner, Jr., *To the Hartford Convention: The Federalists and the Origins of Party Politics in Massachusetts, 1789–1815* (New York: Alfred A. Knopf, 1970), and Robert Dawidoff, *The Education of John Randolph* (New York: W. W. Norton, 1979).

Robert E. Shalhope has correctly pointed out that republicanism is best viewed as a political culture that people understood and acted within, not as a singular cause of their actions in every instance—see his two articles in the *William and Mary Quarterly*, "Toward a Republican Synthesis: The Emergence of an Understanding of Republicanism in American Historiography," 3d ser., 29 (1972): 49–80, and "Republicanism and Early American Historiography," 3d ser., 39 (1982): 334–56. Shalhope's articles are an essential starting point for reading about the "republican synthesis" because they help the reader to identify sub-themes within the overall interpretive framework, even as they annotate the major books and articles on the topic. One of Shalhope's recent points—his enthusiasm for Kenneth Burke's work in symbolic action and the promise that this interpretation holds for studies of political action in the early Republic—is deserving of more extended comment.

Burke's writing, although seminal, is in a style that sometimes makes it obscure to the point of frustration. Yet the reward for patience is an enriched sense of the dynamic interplay between language and reality. For an overview of his treatment of symbolic forms and functions, see "Dramatism" in *Communication: Concepts and Perspectives*, ed. Lee Thayer (Washington, D.C.: Spartan Books, 1967), pp. 327–53. A set of "summarizing essays" appears in *Language as Symbolic Action: Essays on Life, Literature, and Meth-*

od (Berkeley and Los Angeles: Univ. of California Press, 1968), two
of which are especially helpful: "Definition of Man," pp. 3–24, and
"Terministic Screens," pp. 44–62. Burke's major books also include
A Rhetoric of Motives (1950; rpt. Berkeley and Los Angeles: Univ.
of California Press, 1969), in which he examines how humans are
induced to cooperate with one another through rhetorical forms
that serve as strategies of identification. His method for analyzing
the motivational structure of symbolic acts is presented in *A Gram-
mar of Motives* (1945; rpt. Berkeley and Los Angeles: Univ. of California Press, 1969). *Performance and Change: An Anatomy of Purpose* (1935; rpt. Indianapolis: Bobbs-Merrill, 1965), one of Burke's
earliest books, continues to be among the clearest and most useful
introductions to his general perspective. *Attitudes Toward History*
(1937; rpt. Boston: Beacon, 1961) is a valuable study of how symbols, throughout the curve of history, have organized the attitudes
of political communities into frames of acceptance and rejection.
The Philosophy of Literary Form (1941; rpt. Berkeley and Los Angeles: Univ. of California Press, 1973) includes an explicit discussion
of Burke's method for tracking down the strategic uses of symbols
and an exemplary essay on Hitler's rhetoric in *Mein Kampf*. Burke's
basic definition of symbolic form, as the creation and fulfillment of
expectations, and his system for classifying rhetorical appeals appear in *Counter-Statement* (1931; rpt. Berkeley and Los Angeles:
Univ. of California Press, 1968). Throughout these several works,
Burke explores the implications of being separated from our natural
environment by instruments of our own making, i.e., by symbols. As
he puts the matter, "Even if any given terminology is a *reflection* of
reality, by its very nature as a terminology it must be a *selection* of
reality; and to this extent it must function also as a *deflection* of
reality" ("Terministic Screens," p. 45).

Themes related to and often based upon Burke's ideas have
emerged in several disciplines. Hugh Dalziel Duncan's *Communication and Social Order* (New York: Oxford Univ. Press, 1968) bridges
sociology and literature. Victor Turner's *Dramas, Fields, and Metaphors: Symbolic Action in Human Society* (Ithaca: Cornell Univ.
Press, 1974) represents an anthropological approach. Much of current thinking about the impact of social interaction on definitions of
reality is reflected in Peter L. Berger and Thomas Luckman, *The
Social Construction of Reality* (Garden City, N.Y.: Doubleday,

1967). Three books by Murray Edelman offer valuable insights into the political implications of symbolic action: *The Symbolic Uses of Politics* (Urbana: Univ. of Illinois Press, 1964); *Politics as Symbolic Action: Mass Arousal and Quiescence* (Chicago: Markham, 1971); and *Political Language: Words that Succeed and Policies that Fail* (N.Y.: Academic Press, 1977). Doris A. Graber summarizes research on language in politics with her *Verbal Behavior and Politics* (Urbana: Univ. of Illinois Press, 1976) and "Political Languages," in *Handbook of Political Communication*, eds. Dan D. Nimmo and Keith R. Sanders (Beverly Hills: Sage Publications, 1981), pp. 195–223. Another essay of note in the *Handbook of Political Communication* is "A Process Approach," pp. 39–65, by James E. Combs. See also Combs's *Dimensions of Political Drama* (Santa Monica, Cal.: Goodyear Publishing Co., 1980). A particularly useful discussion of alternative views of metaphor and its role in shaping political realities is presented by Eugene F. Miller, "Metaphor and Political Knowledge," *American Political Science Review* 73 (1979): 155–70. For a broader treatment of Miller's topic, applied to rhetorical forms in general, see Robert L. Scott, "On Viewing Rhetoric as Epistemic," *Central States Speech Journal* 18 (1967): 9–17, and his sequel, "On Viewing Rhetoric as Epistemic: Ten Years Later," *Central States Speech Journal* 27 (1976): 258–66. The relevance of Scott's theme to major trends in rhetorical scholarship is reflected in Michael C. Leff's "In Search of Ariadne's Thread: A Review of the Recent Literature on Rhetorical Theory," *Central States Speech Journal* 29 (1978): 73–91. Among the more influential essays (of the several that continue to appear in journals such as *Philosophy and Rhetoric, Communication Monographs*, and the various regional journals affiliated with the Speech Communication Association) is Ernest G. Bormann's "Fantasy and Rhetorical Vision: The Rhetorical Criticism of Social Reality," *Quarterly Journal of Speech* 58 (1972): 396–407. An excellent critique of Bormann's influential ideas for applying rhetoric to the study of symbolic action in historical as well as contemporary settings is G. P. Mohrmann's "An Essay on Fantasy Theme Criticism," *Quarterly Journal of Speech* 68 (1982): 109–32. Perhaps the most comprehensive discussion of rhetoric, per se, in a manner readily adaptable to studies in symbolic action, is Chaim Perelman and L. Olbrechts-Tyteca, *The New Rhetoric: A Treatise on Argumentation*, trans. John Wilkinson and Purcell Weaver (Notre Dame: Univ. of Notre Dame Press, 1969). A concise statement of the thesis of their book is made in the first chapter of Chaim Perelman, *The New Rhetoric and the Humanities: Essays on Rhetoric and Its Applications* (Dordrecht, Holland: D. Reidel Publishing Co., 1979).

By no means is this a comprehensive list of the important work relevant to symbolic action. It is meant only to reflect some of the diversity of ideas available to anyone interested in pursuing the subject further. Additional references might be made to George Herbert Mead's *Mind, Self, and Society* and the symbolic interactionists who have followed his lead, to Quincy Wright's discussion of symbols in his massive *A Study of War*, to Kenneth Boulding's influential book *The Image* and several of his related works, to Susan Langer's *Philosophy in a New Key*, to Clifford Geertz and his treatment of ideology as a cultural system, and to many others. Each of the suggestions will guide the interested reader down additional avenues of thought and lead to other valuable references.

Finally, a comment is in order about our use of quantitative methods and theories of human behavior derived from the social sciences. There have been several thoughtful articles in recent years tallying the assets and debits of this research. Lawrence Stone in his article, "The Revival of Narrative: Reflections on a New Old History," *Past and Present* 85 (1979): 3–24, senses that narrative history is on the upswing again, and many like Robert P. Swierenga are assessing the gains of the movement in modest, rather than revolutionary, terms: "Behavioralism in Historical Research," *Conspectus in History* 1 (1978): 75–88.

We share with Konrad H. Jarausch the belief that the difference between qualitative and quantitative history is not as great as was once thought. "In the final analysis," Jarausch concludes, "quantitative history must meet the same tests as any other systematic scholarly reconstruction of the past—namely of accuracy, imaginativeness, and logic, in short, of quality" (*AHA Perspectives* Vol. 20, no. 8[1982]: 21). All students of the U.S. Congress, or of decision making in any group, have essentially the same task: at some point words and actions—ideas and behavior—have to be reconciled. This book, we hope, is another step in that direction.

Index